Destined to become an inspirational classic . . .

**HOW TO WIN OVER DEPRESSION**
**by**
**Dr. Tim LaHaye**

A book to help you understand and overcome one of life's most mysterious and universal problems.

Bantam Books by Dr. Tim LaHaye

THE ACT OF MARRIAGE (with Beverly LaHaye)
HOW TO WIN OVER DEPRESSION

# HOW TO WIN OVER DEPRESSION

## Dr. Tim LaHaye

BANTAM BOOKS
TORONTO · NEW YORK · LONDON · SYDNEY

HOW TO WIN OVER DEPRESSION
*A Bantam Book / published by arrangement with
The Zondervan Corporation*

*PRINTING HISTORY*
*Zondervan edition published January 1974
13 printings through June 1976
Bantam edition / August 1976*
2nd printing ........ March 1977    3rd printing .... February 1979
4th printing ............ August 1980

*Bantam Books are published by Bantam Books, Inc. Its trade-
mark, consisting of the words "Bantam Books" and the por-
trayal of a bantam, is Registered in U.S. Patent and Trademark
Office and in other countries. Marca Registrada. Bantam
Books, Inc., 666 Fifth Avenue, New York, New York 10103.*

PRINTED IN THE UNITED STATES OF AMERICA

13 12 11 10 9 8 7 6 5 4

*This book is dedicated to the depressed. For all those who have needlessly suffered the misery of hopelessness and despair, expecting no escape from this dreaded emotional epidemic, it is the author's hope they will not only read the suggested cures found here, but follow the remedies to a new way of life.*

# Contents

| | | |
|---|---|---|
| | *Acknowledgments* | ix |
| | *Introduction* | xi |
| 1. | The Problem of Depression | 1 |
| 2. | Struggles Against Depression | 7 |
| 3. | The Symptoms of Depression | 15 |
| 4. | The Cycles of Depression | 21 |
| 5. | The Causes of Depression | 39 |
| 6. | Is There a Cure for Depression? | 51 |
| 7. | The Place of Anger in Depression | 79 |
| 8. | Self-Pity and Depression | 89 |
| 9. | How to Overcome Self-Pity | 105 |
| 10. | Depression and Your Mind | 117 |
| 11. | Depression and Your Self-Image | 131 |
| 12. | Depression and Your Temperament | 153 |
| 13. | Depression and the Occult | 173 |
| 14. | Depression and Music | 181 |
| 15. | Ten Steps to Victory Over Depression | 187 |
| 16. | How to Help Your Children Avoid Depression | 207 |
| 17. | How to Help a Depressed Friend | 219 |
| 18. | The Miserable Majority | 225 |
| 19. | An Eighty-Five-Year-Old Optimist | 233 |
| | *Bibliography* | 239 |

# Acknowledgments

The author is indebted to many people for assistance in the writing of this book. Many depressed counselees have provided insights into the problem of depression and given me ample opportunity to test the validity of the formulas for victory over depression found here.

Dr. James DeSaegher, a member of the English department of United States International University, San Diego, has helped immeasurably in the grammatical preparation of the manuscript. Mrs. Barrie Lyons, Linda Dukes and Mrs. Bonnie Perry have typed and transcribed my hastily scrawled notes or dictation done primarily while flying en route to speaking engagements. Doctors William Halcomb of San Clemente, Nelson Bell and William McCandless of San Diego, along with Nurse Ruth Erne, have advised me on the medical aspects of the subject, carefully reviewing the first six chapters. Airline stewardesses, businessmen and passengers who engaged me in conversation after noting the subject matter on which I was writing have voiced positive comment and convinced me this book was sorely needed.

Finally, my wonderful wife and children who have so graciously indulged my mental preoccupation during the months of its creation have earned my heartfelt gratitude.

# Introduction

When *Newsweek* magazine devoted its cover page and a lead article to "Coping With Depression," that was the last straw! For some time I had contemplated writing a book on "How to Win Over Depression," but that article finally motivated me. When I read, "For there is no doubt that depression, long the leading mental illness in the U.S., is now virtually epidemic—and suicide is its all too frequent outcome,"[1] it confirmed my own observations. If my counseling room was any indication, depression was on the rise. That article and the recent surge of books on the subject indicate that our city has no corner on a problem that is sweeping western civilization.

For several years I have made a special study of this life-destroying emotional malady. In my training and research I was confronted with a mass of confusion, contradiction and psychologically disguised suggestions that were hard to pin down. As the flow of depressed persons began to increase, I was forced to help them as best I could. Gradually, a therapeutic formula was developed which many found beneficial. Occasionally I had thought about writing this book in the hope that readers could likewise benefit from the formula, but my intention was not seriously motivated until a little more than three years ago.

Not usually prone to depression, I could not read-

---

[1]"Coping With Depression," Copyright *Newsweek*, LXXXI (January 8, 1973), 51. Reprinted by permission.

ily identify from personal experience with the emotional disturbances of my counselees. But on October 7, 1969, I experienced the most devastating event of my life since my father died when I was ten years old. Struck by my first serious wave of depression, I could for the first time truly identify with the cold, apathetic, hopeless feeling of the depressed.

The first depression passed within a few days, but during the next two and a half years I experienced four more depressions, all stemming from the same source. Looking back, I find that each time I used the formula given to others, the depression passed. It returned whenever I failed to heed the formula.

Now that depression has reached "virtually epidemic" proportions nationally, and now that I know something about it by personal experience, both through success and failure, I think it is time to publish this book. Hopefully it will help many others realize the true cause of a major emotional culprit and offer a workable remedy.

Of one thing I am confident: you do not have to be depressed. If you or someone you love has this problem, you will welcome the good news of a means to gain victory over it. I am convinced that by using the formula in this book, you can avoid ever being depressed again.

# 1

# The Problem of Depression

An attractive woman in her mid-thirties sat in my counseling room and heaved that long and somewhat discouraging sigh I had come to associate with the depressed. Her name could have been "Mrs. Everything"—you name it, she had it.

Leaving her $65,000 ranch-style home and a wardrobe filled with mod clothes, she drove her troubles to my office in a new station wagon. She had three lovely school-age daughters and a dynamic executive-type husband who had "never been unfaithful." Even though she possessed almost everything she wanted, she was not happy.

Three times a week for two months she had been seeing a psychiatrist, yet only two nights before coming to me Mrs. Everything had almost taken her life. In a state of depression she had lowered the shades in her bedroom, had crawled back into bed as soon as the girls had left for school, and had pulled the sheets up over her head. Her well-groomed appearance to the contrary, she claimed that she had climbed out of such a bed to visit my office.

Although that young mother's case of depression was severe, it was not the worst I had ever seen. In fact, her emotional condition was not at all uncom-

1

mon, for the majority of people I counsel are depressed. In talking to other counselors, I find this to be general rule. On almost any day the average counselor is confronted with several cases of depression. A prominent psychologist recently observed, "Every one of us is depressed at times. It is perfectly normal." A medical doctor, lecturing to other doctors on how to diagnose depression, commented, "In a sense, depression should be expected in every individual."

For many years depression has been the nation's number one emotional illness and it is on the increase. At more than forty Family Life Seminars I have conducted in various parts of the country, my cassette lecture on "The Cause and Cure of Depression" has without exception sold more than any other lecture— even more than "Sexual Harmony in Marriage," "Overcoming Worry," "Why Opposites Attract Each Other," and ten other selections.

Between 50,000 and 70,000 people commit suicide each year, and we know that only a small percent of those who attempt suicide actually succeed. Investigation has revealed that more than half of those people were suffering from depression. The National Institute of Mental Health indicates that 125,000 Americans are hospitalized annually with depression, whereas another 200,000 or more are treated by psychiatrists. Dr. Nathan Kline of New York's Rockland State Hospital reports that many unrecognized cases of depression go untreated. Estimates reach as high as four to eight million annually.[1] In the opinion of many researchers, more human suffering results from depression than from any other disease affecting mankind.

Although increasing at an alarming rate, depression is not new. History and literature clearly indicate that it is as ancient as man. The oldest book known, the Book of Job, introduces a great man in a serious state of depression, exclaiming, "So am I made to possess months of vanity, and wearisome nights are appointed to me. When I lie down, I say, When shall I arise, and

---

[1] "Coping With Depression," p. 51.

the night be gone? and I am full of tossings to and fro unto the dawning of the day. My flesh is clothed with worms and clods of dust, my skin is broken, and become loathsome. My days are swifter than a weaver's shuttle, and are spent without hope. O remember that my life is wind: mine eye shall no more see good. The eye of him that hath seen me shall see me no more: thine eyes are upon me, and I am not. As the cloud is consumed and vanisheth away: so he that goeth down to the grave shall come up no more. He shall return no more to his house, neither shall his place know him any more. Therefore I will not refrain my mouth; I will speak in the anguish of my spirit; I will complain in the bitterness of my soul."[2] After reading what happened to Job (loss of family and fortune, boils covering his body), who could say that he would not have reacted similarly under like circumstances?

The first writer on record to categorically describe depression was Hippocrates, the Greek physician and philosopher. In his ingenious classification of the four temperaments, he labeled one "melancholia," proposing the erroneous explanation that it was caused by black, heavy blood passing through the patient's veins.

A physician named Aretaeus in the second century described the depressed as "sad" and "dismayed." He suggested that they became thin, agitated, and sleepless. If the condition were allowed to persist, they complained of "a thousand futilities" and desired to die.[3]

Another second-century man, Plutarch, created a distinctly religious context for melancholia: "He looks on himself as a man whom the gods hate and pursue with their anger. A far worse lot is before him; he dares not employ any means of averting or of remedying the evil, lest he be found fighting against the gods. The physician, the consoling friend, are driven away. 'Leave me,' says the wretched man, 'me, the

---

[2] Job 7:3-11.

[3] Aaron T. Beck, *Depression: Causes and Treatment* (Philadelphia: University of Pennsylvania Press, 1967), p. 4.

impious, the accursed, hated of the gods, to suffer my punishment.' He sits out of doors, wrapped in sackcloth or in filthy rags. Ever and anon he rolls himself, naked, in the dirt confessing about this and that sin. He has eaten or drunk something wrong. He has gone some way or other which the divine being did not approve of. The festivals in honor of the gods give no pleasure to him but fill him rather with fear or a fright."[4]

A careful study of these ancients reveals a constant similarity to modern descriptions of depression. Dr. Beck, for instance, explains, "The cardinal signs and symptoms used today in diagnosing depression are found in the ancient descriptions: disturbed mood (sad, dismayed, futile); self-castigations ('the accursed, hated of the gods'); self-debasing behavior ('wrapped in sackcloth or in filthy rags . . . he rolls himself, naked, in the dirt'); wish to die; physical and vegetative symptoms (agitation, loss of appetite and weight, sleeplessness); and delusions of having committed unpardonable sins. The foregoing descriptions of depression include the typical characteristics of this condition. There are few psychiatric syndromes whose clinical descriptions are so constant through successive eras of history."[5]

It is rather embarrassing that to our dismay, unfortunately, after almost 2500 years secular man of our day is not much better able to cure the problem than were the ancients.

## Depression Is Universal

It is safe to say that everyone becomes depressed at some point in his or her life. Oh, he may not be so despairing as to attempt suicide, but he *has* experienced depression at some time or other. During the past few years I have token polls in audiences totaling at least 100,000 people, inquiring, "Is there anyone here who has never experienced depression in his entire life?" So

---

[4]*Ibid.,* p. 5.
[5]*Ibid.*

far not one person has indicated that he has escaped this problem.

Naturally, all of the people were not conceding that they were mired in the Slough of Despond. Many of them were thinking of light stages of depression which they called the "blues," or, as one woman said, "I have the weeps." But they were all conscious that at times in their lives they had been unhappy. Obviously, there is a great difference between unhappiness and mental illness. However, even the mildest form of depression dulls the sharpness of the keen edge of life.

Depression not only is universal, but it also is no respecter of persons. Recent studies show that the poor suffer with it just as much as the rich. As we shall show in this book, it is not caused by circumstances, possessions, or position in life; therefore, all men are susceptible to it.

No profession is exempt from depression, for I have met depressed cab drivers, housewives, businessmen, school teachers, construction workers, and contractors. Many fear that confessing they are depressed is tantamount to acknowledging they have some mental deficiency. Although it is indeed related to thinking patterns, it has nothing to do with I.Q. If anything, people with the highest I.Q. are more vulnerable to this malady. For instance, almost every authority I have consulted in this field refers to the fact that Sir Winston Churchill, a bastion of strength to England at a time of great national crisis, was given to serious bouts of depression. Some of the world's greatest geniuses were plagued with the problem. After a notable work of art or feat of creativity, they fell into an apathetic period of depression.

Most high school students remember the short story by Edgar Allen Poe entitled "The Pit and the Pendulum." It is said that after this product of his genius, the great author fell into a four-day depression. Some, like Stephen Foster, buried their creativity in alcohol; various poets shortened their lives through wanton sex, and other artists wasted their genius in equally bizarre conduct. Van Gogh even cut off his ear in a fit of despair.

When we say that everyone has experienced depression, we are speaking generally of the many forms it takes, which will be dealt with later. These include the "blues" and minor mood swings, common to all individuals, to the most severe psychosis. Life itself is unpredictable, and every human being will necessarily experience unhappiness. One psychiatrist has admitted, "We seem to be starved for happiness most of the time." For most people happiness is a rare commodity which, as we shall see, depends more on mental attitude than on circumstances, but whenever a person is unhappy he has a tendency to feel depressed to some degree. It is unrealistic for any human being to think he can escape life's natural causes of unhappiness. If, therefore, to live is to experience varying degrees of unhappiness, and since depression is the opposite of happiness, then all men are bound on some occasions to feel depressed.

Students of human behavior have long wrestled with two questions: (1) Why are some people more frequently depressed than others? and (2) What is the true cause of depression? Both of these questions will be addressed in subsequent chapters. Many like to think it it a physically induced illness, thus relieving themselves of any responsibility for it. In so doing, they seriously jeopardize their chances of recovery.

I have observed happy and contented people whose joy radiated amid life's most unhappy circumstances, whereas others turned the circumstances of joy into beds of depression. Unless an individual is willing to face the fact that his mental attitude toward the circumstances, not the circumstances, cause his unhappiness and depression, he is in my opinion incurable.

# 2

# Struggles Against Depression

One of the first things a sophomore psychology student learns is that self-preservation is the first law of life. When a person injures an arm, he shields that injury with other parts of his body. If he injures a leg, he will consciously and subconsciously place an additional amount of weight on his good leg. The natural struggle for existence will automatically cause emotional shifting which produces changes in behavior and, in some cases, changes in appearance.

This is particularly true in the area of depression. Subconscious maneuvers are designed in some cases to avoid depression or to extricate one from its grasp. People use different techniques, gradually developing habit patterns that become characteristic of their personality. These defense mechanisms may manifest themselves as a change in mood, altering their relationships with other people. Their attitude toward circumstances may become regressive or narcissistic and, if protracted, will ultimately result in escape from reality. We speak of this as "losing contact with reality." Such a person may be able to hear but seems incapable of movement or speech. Obviously, the severity of the depression will determine the severity of the struggle against it, which in turn produces what we are prone to call abnormal behavior. It is not uncommon for suicide to be the final attempt to rid oneself of the awful tyranny of depression.

The form this struggle takes in a person's life can be seen as early as infancy, as will be shown later. One of the primary causes of depression is separation from a love object, which is what makes a well-fed, dry and comfortable baby begin to cry when its parents leave the room. The contact with the love object—in this case the mother—produces the happiness. Separation begets loneliness, which ultimately results in depression. Consequently, the child's natural struggle against depression causes him to cry. If the mother is immature and becomes irritated at what then seems to be unreasonable behavior on the part of the baby, she may scream at the child, which seriously compounds the problem. In this case we find two immature persons whose struggle against depression is in conflict. The child's insecurity is magnified by the sound of the mother's angry voice, and the mother's intemperate behavior produces guilt and loss of self-image, which will also contribute toward her depression.

The other possibility is that the child's initial cry cannot be accepted by the young mother, prompting her to rush to the child's aid, lovingly pick it up, and thus eliminate her cause for depression. This action, however, ill prepares the child for life, which of necessity forces all people to periodic separations from their love objects. It not only creates a habit pattern of dependency in the child but also makes the mother an unnecessary slave of her infant's expectations. This ultimately becomes a source of irritation to the mother, which may not only produce depression in her life but ultimately, if indulged, will generate feelings of hostility which she cannot indefinitely keep from expressing. The infant will in turn sense this feeling and, as a result, become depressed.

To digress momentarily concerning a cure for this most common problem, I suggest that you compare emotional and mental development to the physical act of learning to walk. Because it is tangible, we seem better able to cope with the physical side of life than the mental or emotional, which is probably why learning to walk affords such a good illustration. When the child begins to walk, of necessity he repeatedly falls down. It doesn't matter how often he fails, and within certain limits it doesn't matter how hard he falls. But it is important that he be given loving approval and encouragement to try again. Ultimately, all normal children learn to walk. Similarly, normal children learn to separate from their parents. We admit that it can be a painful process but it is a necessary part of life. Therefore, a wise parent lovingly and tenderly starts early to train his child to stand on his own emotionally for short periods of time, taking short psychological steps that equip him for the longer steps of separation which eventually become necessary.

Infantile manifestations of the struggle against depression take on behavior patterns which, although associated with children, are neither universal nor necessary.

Naturally, as a person matures physically, his mental and emotional maturity does not maintain consistent growth. In fact, his behavior may fall further and further below the standard of normalcy.

## Exhibitionism

In childhood this problem manifests itself in temper tantrums, showing off, and other forms of attention getting, including withdrawal. It not uncommonly reveals itself in an obsession toward gambling, not only with money but also with one's life. For a teenage boy it may involve recklessly driving a car or motorcycle; for a teenage girl it may include hitchhiking a ride or being promiscuous sexually; for their parents it may encompass a spending spree or a wasteful visit to the gambling tables of Las Vegas. Quite possibly this obsessive compulsion to gamble one's life, reputation, or material assets is a subconscious tempting of fate caused by the feelings of guilt over one's evil thinking patterns, which have been induced by the separation or loss of a love object.

Exhibitionism is almost universally an expression of the struggle against depression. The child who feels he is losing the love or acceptance of his parent will often lash out in vile or profane words. If the parent wisely and lovingly disciplines the child, he not only helps him establish the foundation for self-discipline and self-control, but he aids the child in relieving his guilt complex, which he will certainly feel, having mentally and verbally abused his parents. (Never underestimate a child's intuitive sense of right and wrong.) Unless checked, this spirit of rebellion will turn against society, manifesting itself in obscene words written in public places and in loudly expressed profane and vile utterances usually considered socially unacceptable. As he grows up, it may express itself in devious plots against society, withdrawal from humanity, and eventually suicide.

Sexual promiscuity may likewise reflect the battle against depression. The secure, loved, and accepted woman does not dress in a provocative manner, but subconsciously prefers modest attire. As a counselor I have observed during the protracted period of the mini and micro-mini skirts that a woman's security level could often be measured by the length of her skirt. This is also true of the woman who is insistent upon wearing men's apparel. For some reason she dislikes being a woman (probably because in her childhood the separation from a love object, possibly her father, was interpreted by her as caused by being a girl); therefore, she does everything possible to disguise her femininity. She not only dresses like a man, but she walks like a man, swears like a man, and indulges in many other unladylike practices. If she accepts herself as a woman but not as a person, she will express her struggle against depression by being flirtatious, suggestive, and, in some cases, promiscuous. Studies have indicated that nymphomaniacs are really not oversexed women, but overly insecure women. The sex drive in a woman is not sufficiently strong enough to explain such behavior. Even the most sexually indiscriminate women I have counseled have indicated that it wasn't their sex drive that motivated them, but their tremendous need for love. Sex was the price they paid to gain the love they craved.

Sexual exhibitionism in men does not take the form of indecent exposure as frequently as it does in women, partly because the fashion industry does not cultivate this problem as much and partly because of the man's stronger sex drive. The male ego usually leads a man to find gratification in sexual conquest. The emotionally immature male tends to equate manhood with profane and obscene speech and the number of women he has taken to bed. The emotionally mature male reveals the absence of his struggle against depression by treating women with dignity and respect, confining his expressions of sex to the special object of his love, his wife.

## Clinging

Another common manifestation of the struggle against depression is called "clinging." Most parents have had the emotionally traumatic experience of forcibly extricating themselves from the clinging arms of their child. I shall never forget my five-year-old son's first day in a San Diego kindergarten. He had spent three weeks getting used to a kindergarten environment in Minnesota before we moved to California, and he was very reluctant to enter a new school situation. It was hard enough to forcibly remove his loving, clinging arms from around my neck, but one of my most difficult tasks was to force myself to walk away from him amid his loud and piteous cry, "Daddy, don't leave me!"

The "clinging" process that in some homes occurs every night just before the light is turned out carries over into adulthood. Naturally, it takes on a more sophisticated behavior. In some cases it adopts the form of excessive generosity well above a person's means. This is nothing more than a subconscious attempt to buy the love of his love object. It may also take the form of making oneself indispensable. Rejection by their boss, or father figure, is so abhorrent to some insecure men that they work long hours and neglect their family. Occasionally one will encounter a compulsive hostess who at first seems to be the "hostess with the mostest," but in reality is clinging avidly to her friends. By wining and dining them she seeks to place them in her debt so that hopefully they will not leave her.

This clinging mechanism is sometimes the motivation of women who continue to board children. Their maternal instinct is increased by their insecurity, and they are obsessed with the yearning to be needed. Consequently, they cannot tolerate not having babies or children dependent upon them. Quite possibly this is one area in which the struggle against depression may be helpful to the recipient, for unless the affection is excessive, the experience of being raised in such a home is preferable to that of being raised in an orphanage.

Another stratagem of clinging includes insistent conversation, whether person to person or on the telephone. One doctor friend noted, "Some people have compulsive telephonitis." One final adult form of clinging is helplessness or sickness for effect. Naturally, these are silent cries for help.

## Attack

An intimidating symbol of one's struggle against depression involves attack—either aggression against someone who has rejected him or, more frequently, an attack on himself. The thought pattern usually proceeds as follows: "Since it is my fault that I am rejected, I must not be any good; consequently, I deserve to be punished." And since no one else will do it, the person often punishes himself—a pathetic practice, to say the least.

Although these defense maneuvers ride the waves of an individual's moods, they are bound to affect a person's behavior in direct proportion to the severity of the mood. Therefore, the best way to remedy the situation is not to change the expression but discover what causes the mood, as we shall show in a later chapter. Thought patterns produce feelings, feelings produce actions. Therefore, any permanent reduction in depression must of necessity deal with the problems of thought patterns. Unless the person's thinking pattern changes, this struggle against depression is bound to produce increasing degrees of erratic behavior.

# 3

## The Symptoms of Depression

The tremendous increase in the number of depressed persons today justifies a brief study of the symptoms of the problem. Almost everyone who reads this book has friends or loved ones who manifest these symptoms. If you don't need to recognize them for yourself, then for their sake you should learn to discern these critical signs quickly and offer your love and support in their time of need.

Three stages of depression are acknowledged almost universally by counselors. Most designate them as mild, severe, and serious. We shall label them discouragement, despondency, and despair. In a later chapter we will show how they affect us mentally, emotionally, and physically, but here it is sufficient to say that most depression commences with discouragement, grows into despondency, and, unless the thought pattern is changed, results in despair. Once the line of despair has been crossed, it is possible for the depression to become so acute that the individual loses contact with reality and must be given medical treatment even to stay alive.

The effects of depression are experienced physically, emotionally, and mentally. The layman recognizes the physical symptoms first, but the specialist can often detect the mental symptoms before they become physical. Unfortunately, the depressed are not usually brought to his attention until they manifest physical symptoms. Too many physical symptoms of depression exist for us to consider in this brief book, so we shall review only the most common.

(1) *Erratic sleep behavior*—The most common physical symptom of depression is a marked change in sleep patterns. Although some depressed people oversleep and awake tired, it is usually more common that they can't sleep at all. If they do, they will awaken in the early hours of the morning and cannot go back to sleep. In a taped panel discussion on depression, several medical doctors agreed that the first red flag to look for in insomnia patients is depression.

(2) *Apathy—lethargy—the blahs*—Another common symptom of depression is reflected in the statements "I feel tired all the time," or "I don't even feel like enjoying my favorite hobby." Depressed people tend to awaken tired and remain unmotivated. Although they are capable of fulfilling their responsibilities, their work performance leaves much to be desired. In addition, they tire easily. One man complained, "My feet feel like they're set in concrete."

(3) *Loss of appetite*—Food loses its charm for the depressed. He listlessly plays with his food, which seems tasteless to him. The more severe the depression, the less the appetite grows. Consequently, if his problem is not checked, he may experience a serious weight loss, which will compound his difficulty. Sometimes the first stages of depression result in constant raiding of the refrigerator for snacks, but usually those in despair can persist for days without food.

(4) *Loss of sex drive*—All drive functions or basic activities come to a standstill when one is depressed. This includes even the sex drive, particularly in women. Some women have been known to get so depressed that even their menstrual function stops. Except in mild depression, when a man may become sexually aggressive because of the threat to his ego, most men lose interest in sex when they are depressed.

(5) *Unkempt appearance*—Whenever a fashionable friend loses interest in his appearance, look for depression. The loss of motor drive, due to the negative self-image of the depressed person, makes a man less concerned with shaving and neatness and causes a woman to skip her hairdresser's appointment. The unkempt attire is a reflection of the way the individual sees himself. Clothes are revealing! They often broadcast a person's concept of himself. He probably is covering up an inferiority complex if overdressed. If well-dressed, he often is communicating a satisfied self-image. However, if he dresses sloppily, when neatness is called for, it usually is because he has given up on himself.

(6) *Many physical ailments*—It is quite common for depressed persons to suffer from many physical maladies, both real and imagined. Some of the common problems are tiredness, weakness, aching, dizziness, heart palpitation, tightening of the chest, trouble with breathing, headache, constipation, heartburn, and sweating.

## The Emotional Symptoms of Depression

Although depression begins in the mind, it will deeply affect a person's emotions. The following are among the most common.

(1) *Loss of affection*—The almost universal tendency of depressed people to withdraw from others is a result of their loss of affection. It begins with a lessening of their love for their spouse or children and grows until they really do not care about themselves, about others or about anything. This is a most harmful emotional state, induced by a faulty thinking pattern of self-occupation. Unless it is changed the depression will increase. Someone has cautioned, "Love or perish." Unless you love others and yourself, you will destroy yourself.

(2) *Sadness*—Joylessness and gloom become a way of life to the depressed. It is so deeply etched on

the table of his heart that it shows on his face. You will look in vain for a smile on the face of the depressed. When he is discouraged, joy and merriment fail to bring him pleasure. As the depression increases, he loses all ability to respond to humor and may become resentful at the joy of those around him.

(3) *The weeps*—A frequent symptom of the depressed is an involuntary tendency to cry. Even those who haven't cried in years may burst into tears or wish to cry but cannot. One woman admitted, "I can always tell when I'm going to be depressed—I get the weeps."

(4) *Hostility*—As we shall see in a later chapter, every case of depression includes a component of anger, at least in the initial stages. At first it is directed at the person who has rejected or insulted him. Later it is turned inward at himself because he caused the rejection. It is not uncommon to hear a depressed person mutter, "I hate myself," or "I get so disgusted with myself."

(5) *Irritability*—Passive people are easily irritated, particularly by those with energy and vitality. They resent individuals who feel good, resist those who try to activate them, and may lash out furiously at routine household noises. Music that normally soothes them may produce discomfort. They can even become agitated at the solicitations of their friends, for they don't feel worthy of someone else's time and concern.

(6) *Anxiety, fear, and worry*—The feelings of loneliness and despair that grow during depression lower the fear threshold. Everything becomes an excuse to worry. The individual will fear being left alone, although he may disguise it. He will flee the past and shrink from the future. Not uncommon is a strong apprehension of death.

(7) *Hopelessness*—Most depressed people are overcome by a sense of hopelessness. They feel trapped by the circumstances that brought on the depression and can envision no way out. Their past is filled with rejection and grief, their present becomes anguish personified, and their gloomy outlook on the future contemplates no solution. Unless someone can inject hope

into their thinking apparatus, the depression will gradually deepen. Typical in the counseling room is the lament, "I am totally discouraged, and no hope is in sight!"

# 4

# The Cycles of Depression

## Moods and Cycles of Depression

Before the days of the automatic washer and dryer, women commonly referred to Monday as "blue Monday." However, that epithet was nothing more than the result of an improper thinking pattern. Most homemakers looked forward with anticipation to the weekend, when the entire family would be home, obviously a time of great joy and satisfaction. But Monday was different; it became a wearisome day to be dreaded. It was not only the first day of routine living again, but the day when most wives did the weekly washing. The thought pattern of dread produced "blue Monday." However, the blues that made Monday an undesirable day had nothing to do with the weather; merely the anticipation of drudgery made it the most tedious day in the week.

This regular pattern of "blue Monday" only illustrates the fact that man's mind is highly suggestible and can fashion a variety of moods. Many things can affect our moods: the weather, the time of year, politics, social events, and a host of other things. Certainly color and music are important factors. One lady I know picked out the color scheme for her home when she was in a bad mood. Shortly after painting the inside of her home, she came in for counseling regarding "the increasing severity of depression." When I found that her color scheme combined various shades of blues and grays, I suggested that she redecorate the house, using bright colors of yellow, white, or pink, colors which communicate warmth, light, and life.

Recently the *Newsweek* article previously mentioned touched on the seasonal problem of depression.

"This is the time of year when the affliction cuts deepest in those who are prone to it: the holidays are over, gone, and the bright promise of Christmas, often painfully unfulfilled, has given way to the bleak reality of the winter that lies ahead. Psychiatrists' telephones jangle with calls for help. An executive oppressed by the incessant gabble of his children has begun drinking heavily. A young housewife, physically exhausted by weeks of anticipatory tension, by gift buying and meal planning, suddenly finds herself in the grip of insomnia. A widow, alone in a small apartment, is racked by protracted fits of sobbing. Now the days are gray, the nights long, and spring is far away.

"Psychiatrists are so familiar with the phenomenon of post-Christmas depression that they have given it a name: the Holiday Paradox. There are a number of obvious reasons why the depression occurs. The holiday season inexorably stirs up deep-seated childhood and family associations and traumas. The exchange of gifts revives the stabbing pain of sibling resentments over who got the most or the best. The holidays are also often a time of reassessment, when the expectations of a youthful past are compared with the realities of adulthood, often with painful results. 'The holidays,' says Dr. Arthur Prange, Jr., of the University of North Carolina, 'are organized to guarantee disappointment.'

"Even the most well-adjusted personalities suffer the pangs of the Holiday Paradox at one time or another—and then go on to an uneventful recovery. But for those predisposed to depression, the holidays can be tragic, even fatal. Although December and January do not rank high as suicide months, suicides do peak sharply just after Christmas Day and New Year's. 'The really bad depressions and suicides hit on the second, third and fourth of January,' says Dr. Robert Litman, co-director of the Los Angeles Suicide Prevention Center. 'It's the worst week of the Year.' "[1]

Not only are depressive moods seasonal, but they can be induced in a whole population as a result of world events. This was graphically illustrated in America during the Vietnam war when the country was fraught with a disillusioned spirit of despondency over the atrocities, the seemingly needless suffering, and the imprisonment of P.O.W.s. A welcome contrast was felt by the entire nation shortly after the peace treaty when news of prisoner releases was announced. A feeling of optimism and well-being filled the country as these heroic men were seen tearfully and joyfully reunited with their families. The contrast in national mood was perceptible in a matter of weeks.

Such mood fluctuations vary in intensity and length depending upon the conditions involved. Most people are more susceptible to low moods after suffering emotional or physical stress and particularly when they are tired. When people do not eat properly (either too much in the evening or the wrong kind of foods), work too hard, or stay up too late, they are more vulnerable to low moods. In marriage counseling I always advise couples against talking about anything negative, particularly in the area of family finances, after 9:30 P.M. It is amazing how much larger our problems seem when we are tired.

Low moods seem to warrant no exceptions. Even the most sanguine person, valued for his good humor and cheerful spirit, will occasionally feel down. In women this is frequently attributed to their menstrual cycle, which takes a toll on them physically and often drains them of needed vitality. However, we should recognize that men also pass through a mood cycle on a regular basis. With women it seems to be every twenty-six to twenty-nine days, but some feel that in

---

[1]"Coping With Depression," p. 51.

men it is more likely to occur every thirty-four to thirty-eight days. Since the male cycle does not include the physical causes for loss of vitality in women, it is not usually as pronounced through nevertheless disturbing.

Analytically gifted people have reported an annual low-mood cycle. One national youth worker has charted his so that he anticipates it every year and prepares himself mentally, emotionally, physically, and spirtually to either offset it or shorten it.

"Sydney J. Harris, syndicated columnist, reports that nothing seems to account for his moods; they just come. Since he has learned this, he anticipates them and does not let them upset him. He sits them out quietly and thus 'cancels the harm they can do.' He confesses that sometimes in the depth of a low mood he thinks his writing is so poor that he hopes the editor will throw it in the waste basket. 'Actually,' he adds, 'the columns I knock out when I am feeling bad are often better than the ones I write in a good mood.' He concludes that a depressed person cannot judge his own work accurately."[2]

Learning to live with and win over one's vacillating moods and periods of depression is the primary concern of this book. I am convinced that if we understand the problem, we can take deliberate steps to avoid becoming its incessant victim. Although low moods do not always produce depression, we are more vulnerable to depression during those periods.

During a low mood, things that ordinarily are absorbed and cause no emotional distress suddenly become a source of irritation that brings on depression. The more we know about the function of human nature, the better able we are to cope with both its positive and negative tendencies. This is particularly true when we apply its general principles to ourselves so that instead of resorting to some of the reactive defense mechanisms that produce abnormal behavior covered in the preceding chapter, we can take positive pre-

---

[2]Kenneth Hildebrand, *Achieving Real Happiness* (New York: Harper and Brothers, 1955), p. 139.

ventive measures as we detect the symptoms. For example, when we are blue, we accentuate the mood by giving in to it. As William James, the psychologist, stated, "The physical expression of an emotion deepens the emotion; while the refusal of expression diminishes the emotion."[3]

This would suggest that whistling or singing when one first recognizes the blues could conceivably chase them away, whereas the downcast, pessimistic outlook would perpetuate them. The psalmist must have had this in mind when he experienced the sense of exaltation I can have when I "lift up mine eyes unto the hills,"[4] even when I do not feel like it. The downward look is merely self-defeating.

## Cycles

Not only is everyone subject to mood swings within the framework of his temperament, personality, life circumstances, and mental attitudes, but he also is liable to cycles of depression. That is, during certain cycles in life people are more susceptible to depression than during others. Human individuality will cause one person to bypass such a period, whereas another may be engulfed by it. Allowing for these individual characteristics, the cycles can be separated into the decades of life. Naturally, everyone does not experience all of the cycles, but because of the changes in life styles and stresses these decades produce, they *may* occur.

## The First Decade of Life

The initial decade in a child's life is usually very happy, unless, of course, he comes from a broken home where, instead of enjoying the security of his parents' presence, he is subjected to separation and insecurity. These are without doubt the most important years of a child's character building and establishment of those elements that produce emotional maturity. One educa-

---

[3]*Ibid.*, p. 141.
[4]Psalm 121:1.

tor submitted that fifty percent of a child's character and personality development take place by the time he is three years old, seventy-five percent by the time he is five years old. The child that is treated to love, discipline, integrity, responsibility, and good examples by his parents during this decade is rich indeed!

## The Second Decade of Life

The first two or three years of the second decade are pleasant for most children, although they soon erupt into what for many is the most traumatic period of their entire life—adolescence. It is marked by emotional instability because an early teenager feels and acts like a child one minute, like an adult the next. His behavior seems almost spontaneous and in some cases out of control. He not only embarrasses and rejects himself, but he also tends to alienate himself from others. One famous children's worker said of junior high young people, "They get to a place where only their mother and father can love them, and sometimes the father wonders how the mother can put up with them." Their excessive behavior induced by their emotional volatility not only makes them insecure about themselves, but causes them to react seriously to the rejection of those they love. Their reaction to this rejection is usually one of hostility, reflected in an argumentative spirit, rebellious attitude, sullenness, or obnoxious behavior, which makes them more unlikable and heightens the rejection, producing more hostile behavior which may lead to their first real experience with depression.

Teenagers also experience difficulty in their blossoming sexual development, which creates new drives they often find difficult to control. Since society and moral principles require that they regulate these drives and their accompanying behavior, teenagers often develop a problem of guilt that produces depression. Guilt is occasioned because they either kick over the traces and violate moral principles or indulge in sexual illusions that lead to masturbation, for which they are later ashamed.

Another cause of adolescent depression is the increasing consciousness of ultimate separation from parents and loved ones. As we have seen, this seems to be the first emotional pressure spot in an infant's life, one that every mature person must ultimately learn to cope with. Some in their late teens escape the seriousness of the problem by becoming emotionally attached to another love object of the opposite sex (usually near their own age), which becomes a stronger desire than that of staying with their parents. This emotional involvement is often called "love," which frequently is interpreted to mean that the couple is ready for marriage. All too often the experience is based on little more than emotional need, fanned by association and passion.

Having been involved in the field of education for several decades, I have been privileged to watch a number of high school young people year after year go through a rather short-term depression that is almost predictable. On the night of graduation they are subject to a euphoric, blissful ecstasy that causes uninhibited weeping and laughing, an emotional reaction often bordering on hysteria, as they say good-by to teachers and friends. Frequently such an experience is followed by a state of depression within one to ten days. This, like other depression syndromes, often can be attributed to the removal of a goal—in this instance, graduation. Unless the young person has sufficient goals that go beyond graduation day, he is prone to experience a severe letdown that produces apathy. The young person who begins a job he relishes the day after graduation tends to escape the problem, as does the young lady who immediately plunges into plans for her impending wedding.

## The Third Decade of Life

Depression in the third decade usually is associated with marriage, particularly in the case of married women whose primary mental attention is fixed on the home during this period. Married men in their twenties are more prone to give their attention to education or vocational endeavors, thus remaining mentally stimulated. In addition, their youthful energies usually keep them athletically active. Therefore, they do not normally experience as much depression as women in this third decade of life.

Brides frequently give in to depression either shortly after the wedding or upon returning from the honeymoon. There are many reasons for this. One is the psychological letdown that routine living often produces when contrasted with the exciting preparation prior to the wedding. Another cause for this depression is that her dreams and expectations were so idealistic that real experience becomes disillusioning. This is particularly true if she encounters severe discomfort in intercourse. Some girls find that the consummation of the act of marriage is somewhat painful and unfulfilling. Instead of recognizing that this is a common experience that will soon be overcome by repetition, she may build up a fear or dream of the experience which will destroy the couple's relationship. This often leads to depression. Couples have come to my office within four days after their marriage, but usually their problems are resolved within a short time if both parties are loving and considerate of each other's needs.

If the young bride escapes post-wedding depression, she may experience it after the birth of her first baby. Psychologists call this "postpartum depression." Most women sustain a letdown after childbirth, but not necessarily after each child. Although a depressed-prone woman is more likely to have this experience, it is not uncommon for a sanguine mother to be weepy for several days after childbirth. This can be explained by the separation of the child from the mother or by the severe emotional strain the mother undergoes at childbirth. In some cases this depression becomes protracted and serious if the mother looks upon the child as an intruder. More than one young woman who later went on to be fine, loving mothers indicated that their depression became so severe that they were afraid they might do something harmful to their child. This is usually a temporary malady.

Occasionally young fathers experience a mild depression induced by having to share the love and attention of their wife with the "little stranger" and by becoming sharply aware of the increased financial responsibility. More intense periods of depression will usually occur on the first or fifteenth of the month!

If the couple has two or three small children close together, it is not uncommon for the mother in the late part of the third decade to experience depression and frigidity. This is simply her reaction to confinement with small children and an aversion to feeling like a prisoner. Her frigidity is not caused by a lessening of her desire for the love of her husband, but by the fact that her subconscious fear of pregnancy overpowers it. In addition, heavy demands are made upon her emotionally, and she may be physically exhausted from the two or three childbirths and the tremendous work load her children entail. If she begins to feel sorry for herself in such circumstances, she will soon experience serious problems with depression, which may cause her to lose interest in her appearance, creating a loss of self-image and thus increasing depression. She also risks the chance that her husband may lessen his concern for her because of her unkempt appearance. Incidentally, since men are stimulated by sight, a young mother should make sure that the best-looking woman her husband sees all day is his wife when he opens the door at night. This spruce-up just before five o'clock is not only good for him, but also very beneficial to her own sense of self-worth.

Still another occasion for depression may occur in the third decade of life when the last child goes off to school. The mother who felt so needed by her pre-school child no longer sustains that need from 8:30 A.M. to 3:00 P.M. Consequently, she is vulnerable to depression unless she finds some creative use for her energies.

## The Fourth Decade of Life

Most people function as parents of teenagers during the fourth decade of life. Presently fifty percent of the mothers in this country are homemakers; the others are working wives. Consequently, about half of the mothers of teenagers are very busy women. The father during this time is an active businessman, perhaps an employee on the way up. It is a lively, busy time in the life of a family whose major attention often revolves around the emotionally volatile behavior of teenage children. If the parents have anticipated this period by conferring proper amounts of love and discipline together with moral principles on the child, this can be a happy time. But if they have indulged and pampered their children, they may be confronted with rebellious young people, anxious to develop their lives and impatient with parental restrictions. If so, even the active thirties can produce periods of depression. In spite of the hectic family pace during this stage of life, however, it has a surprisingly low incidence of depression.

## The Fifth Decade of Life

Most psychiatrists agree that an increase in depression is common during the fifth decade of life. Dr. Mortimer Ostow, a neurologist and psychiatrist serving on the staff of Mt. Sinai Hospital in New York City, states, "There is an increase in the frequency of depression and of suicide in the fifth and sixth decades of life. At that time, there may be an initial attack of depression, or a return of depression which first occurred earlier in adult life, or there may simply be an increase in the frequency or depth of a series of depressions which have been recurring for some time.

"I believe that depression at this period in life may be ascribed to the gradual decrease in vital energies which starts relatively early in adult life but which becomes more abrupt in the fifth and sixth decades. It is this decline in energies which produces the temperamental changes that we ordinarily expect in the fifth and sixth decades, namely, mellowness, a decline in ambition, relaxation of aggressiveness, and a lessening of interests in the new together with a heightened attachment to the old.

"I imagine that this change is part of the normal biology of human life. It may be the effect of the reduction of the secretion of gonadal hormones, of pituitary hormones, of secretions of the pineal gland, or simply of aging of the brain, and especially the central and basal sections of the brain called the basal ganglia."[5]

Men probably face the greatest tendency toward depression in this fifth decade. In fact, it is not uncommon for men who have never known depression to experience it for the first time during this period, either vocationally, sexually or both. Vocationally, most men feel like one depressed man who confided to me, "I always said if a man doesn't hit it vocationally by the time he is forty, he never will. I'm forty-five, I haven't hit it yet, and it doesn't look like I ever will." Although his case was more severe than most, the man whose job has lost its challenge or whose early dreams will not be realized may slip into a period of depression. These periods will increase in frequency until he restructures his thinking patterns and finds realistic challenges and goals within the framework of his education, talents and opportunity.

During this period the gradual decrease in his vital energies may cause a drop in his sex drive and performance. It is not uncommon for him to experience his first trace of impotence or difficulty in performance. Because nothing is a greater threat to his male ego, he may begin to fear total impotence and be cast into a state of depression. Such men often begin to chase women in an attempt to reclaim their lost sex drive. Quite possibly that is why the period has earned the title "the foolish forties." The mature man in this state learns to content himself with slightly less frequent relations with his wife than during his twenties. He also discovers that sex is more meaningful and enjoyable as an expression of love rather than an attempt to satisfy his male ego.

Women in their forties also have their particular problems, not the least of which is the graduation of children from the home. In addition, even more frequently than brides experience depression after the ceremony, their mothers are prone to give in to this problem. Adjusting to the loss of a daughter in the home, coupled with a severe drain on her nervous energy caused by the frantic wedding preparations, often leaves her exhausted. The severity and length of depression is determined by her plans from that point on.

When the last young person at home goes off to college, enters the armed services, or marries, mother is faced with a tremendous adjustment period. Unless she gets involved in helping other people and recognizes that she is a productive human being still needed by her fellowman, she will experience frequent periods of depression. Her insecurity may cause her to be more sexually aggressive than usual, and if not afforded the love and acceptance of her husband, which she needs at this time, she may give in to temptations of infidelity unless, of course, she possesses strong moral principles to the contrary. Once yielding to infidelity, she is often buffeted by the guilt neurosis that produces depression.

## The Sixth Decade of Life

It has been my observation that two distinct categories of people live through their sixth and seventh decades of life. The first includes those who have accepted the fact that they are more than halfway through life and have learned to cope with their gradual decrease in vital energies. These individuals enjoy their work, often at an increased tempo, because they know that their accomplishments in life must be achieved quickly. They usually engage in hobbies, particularly golfing, bowling, and the less strenuous activities which tend to give them genuine pleasure. They make friends with others their own age, with whom they have much in common; this creates an enriching way of life. They also have grandchildren by this time, and if they have maintained good rapport with their children, this can develop into an exciting relationship that injects a rewarding dimension into their lives. Consequently, even though they may have experienced waves of depression in the fifth decade of life, they may completely bypass it in the sixth and seventh.

The other group of individuals living during this sixth decade tend to reject the inevitable. Refusing to face the fact that they have reached their fifties, they become depressed. One man who had not learned the beauty of maturity lamented, "I am no longer the man I once was." This form of self-rejection will rapidly cause depression. As a consequence, the depression will tend to make him undesirable, and he will withdraw into a complaining and often neurotic state. It is not uncommon for marriages of over thirty years to go through a period of turbulence initiated either by the narcissistic wife who is afraid of her loss of beauty or the formerly energetic husband who rejects the natural maturing process of life. Fortunately, this is a temporary period of depression for most people; once self-acceptance is achieved and new and realistic goals are projected for the future, the individual's fluctuating moods begin to stabilize.

This is the decade when most women begin their change of life, if they have not already begun in the late forties. Many experts, including a number of women authorities, suggest that the problems of this stage are unrealistically exaggerated. If a woman expects to go to pieces during this period, you can be sure she will. However, if she anticipates taking it in stride with a minimum of discomfort and complaining, it will be much less severe. Unquestionably, her hormonal functions are altered, and she will sense some changes in her emotional responses, the degree of which varies with the individual. But the sooner she learns to cope with hers, the better off she will be. She should certainly consult her physician and read such wholesome material as he recommends. Much of the problem can be resolved not only by medication, but also by exchanging old wives' fables and misconceptions for scientific information.

Women must learn one basic essential: the change of life does not make them sexually inhibited or undesirable. There is strong indication to the contrary that after going through the change of life, many women find the greatest sexual pleasure of their married life. Again, more important than biology is the individual's mental attitude.

## The Seventh Decade of Life

An increasing problem with depression during the seventh decade is caused primarily by the inability of people to cope with retirement or the loss of their mate. Because of the affluence of our society, many people are retiring after their sixtieth or sixty-second birthday. If the individual's goal has been to take his ease, sit in a rocking chair, and do nothing when he reaches this stage, he is likely to become not only a depressed-prone person but also a mortality statistic. Everyone is familiar with the industrious businessman who lived a very productive life but died within eighteen months after his retirement without any real physical defect. In most cases the problem stemmed from the lack of goals and interests he should have projected for his years of retirement. Business firms have found that sixty-five-year-old men should not necessarily retire, for they may yet be able to offer several years of productive contribution to their company. Recently I spoke with a man who sold a multimillion dollar company which he had built over a fifty-year period. At five o'clock in the afternoon I found him still in his office, busily managing the affairs of his life at seventy-five years of age. He is still used as a consultant by his former firm, computers and modern technology notwithstanding.

My uncle, at seventy-five years of age, still refuses to retire as a Baptist minister after fifty-three years of service. In fact, the church he pastors is experiencing the greatest growth level of its one-hundred-year history. Such a man has learned to cope with his maturity and continues to make a much needed contribution to life. Consequently, he is not plagued with depression. It seems that depression-free living during the seventh decade of life is determined by one's contribution to the well-being of other people and society. No person should retire without including that dimension in his thinking. Everyone needs to be needed. I know a happy, well-adjusted seventy-year-old former sea captain who teaches Sunday school and is an active leader with senior citizens.

Beware of the retirement obsession! The human mind can adapt to almost anything, with the exception of idleness. That is doubtless the reason for the ancient Chinese curse, "I hope you are confined to eternal idleness!"

Plan your retirement to be an active and productive time; you will enjoy it longer. Very few people "wear out"—most people "rust out."

## Separation Through Death

The second major problem in this seventh decade of life concerns the difficulty of coping with the loss of one's life companion. Statistically it is said that fifty percent of those over sixty-five are either single, divorced or widowed. Of all the traumatic experiences a person faces in life, the most critical seems to be the loss of a life partner through death.

Many people, particularly those without spiritual reserves, are incapable of making the necessary adjustment to this tragedy. If they refuse to accept it and indulge in self-pity for having been left behind, they will experience increasing periods of depression that can shorten their life. Friends of mine were in their mid-seventies when they celebrated their fifty-sixth wedding anniversary. The husband, who had been ill for about nine months, passed away a few weeks later. His wife, who had faithfully nursed her husband, died two days later for no apparent reason. But she had a reason! She lost her desire to live when she lost her husband. The understandable grief and depression was more than her tired old body could take, and thus their funeral services were held simultaneously.

## The Eighth Decade of Life

The eighth decade is not significantly different from any other except that senility may become a problem which in turn creates depression in the life of a marriage partner. His declining health and an increase in physical maladies is apt to make a person more conscious of himself and his feelings than anything else. If he is depression-prone, this will intensify feelings of hypochondria and make his infirmities worse. In addition, his circle of friends is apt to decline through death, and he cannot keep pace with the energetic society around him.

Preoccupation with self during this period is a natural and dangerous threat to well-being. It is not uncommon for such people to be thrown back on their own responsibility. At a time when they are declining physically and financially, this is a tailor-made environment for self-pity. Their children have families of their own, and the retired senior citizen tends to withdraw into the shell of his apartment and live in the past.

## The Ninth Decade of Life

Surprisingly enough, the ninth decade of life does not seem to be generally infused with the depressions of the other decades. Some suggest that this is because people return to a child-like attitude toward life at this age. Personally, I am inclined to think that it is because the depressed-prone, introspective types have already brought on a premature death and that most people living at this age maintain an optimistic outlook on life.

A lengthy survey was made some years ago among octogenarians. Answering over 300 questions to see what they shared in common, they reflected unusual agreement on only one point: a positive anticipation of the future. Somehow they had learned the secret of enjoying today and looking forward to an equally interesting tomorrow. This seems to be the secret of longevity.

## A Conclusion

In retrospect, we find that each stage of life offers its own potential cause of depression. Yet many people live through them all unscathed. Their lack of depression is not due to lack of problems, however, but to a healthy mental attitude amid whatever stage of life they occupy.

# 5

# The Causes of Depression

In chapter 4 we reviewed some of the general causes of depression according to the decades of life. Obviously these do not include all the reasons even the average person could give for his depression. A number of specific causes arise within every decade. Besides, everyone does not mature at the same rate; consequently the general pattern suggested in that chapter may take place before or after the decade mentioned, or hopefully an individual may elude the stage altogether.

Depression is almost always caused by some external experience. For that reason it is very helpful to become aware of the most common causes of the problem so that if they occur in one's life, he need not be engulfed in the potential depression. As nearly as possible we shall attempt to list them in the order of their importance and frequency.

(1) *Disappointment*—Of the hundreds of depressed cases I have examined, without exception they began with a disappointment or experience in which the individual was displeased. No one becomes depressed when everything is going his way. But to live is to experience the disappointment that something or someone has not performed up to expectations.

The cause of the disappointment can be almost anything. One woman's depression began when her pet rosebush died. Another individual's depression was triggered by an expression of irritation on the part of her husband while Christmas shopping. More than one parent has become depressed over the poor grades of his child, and some children get depressed over the negative reaction of their parents to their grades.

One of the most common sources of disappointment in life is people. Because of pressure, physical exhaustion, or a dozen other reasons, they may become irritable, thoughtless or unkind on a particular occasion. If love for ourselves is greater than love for the individual who insults us, we will take offense, become displeased, and progress quickly along the road to discouragement—the first stage of depression. If the hurt or insult is contemplated and nursed long enough, it will produce vexation and ultimately despair.

The more important the object of the insult, the more grievous the discouragement. Since the need for love is so great in all of us, it follows that the greatest source of discouragement is the rejection of someone we love. The root problem with those caught in despair is almost always the rejection of the person they love most.

A recent newspaper article recalled the experience of a schoolteacher father whose wife suddenly divorced him and remarried. He had been so occupied with his work that he had overlooked his wife's discontent with their relationship. He testified, "It took me almost a year to get over it! I had never been depressed in my life until my wife left me. Suddenly the carpet was jerked out from under my whole life. For weeks I just wanted to die." I have seen the most self-sufficient of men lapse into depression after such an experience.

A singular love object often triggers depression in children—namely, the parent. Whether the child's perspective is real or imagined, once he suspects that his parents do not approve of him or, worse yet, wish they had never given birth to him, he becomes a likely subject for depression. Loving encouragement with an ample administration of discipline when needed is a parent's most profitable investment in the life of his child.

Loneliness is not a cause of depression, but a result. The individual whose love object has rejected him, or has been snatched from him by death, will be plunged into depression-producing loneliness. This psychic pain occasioned by the emptiness of loneliness can be healed only by the love of another person. Unfortunately, the depressed person is apt to withdraw from people who in turn are so interested in themselves that they tend to be insensitive to the love needs of others.

(2) *Lack of self-esteem*—Another almost universal characteristic of the depressed person is his lack of self-esteem. Unfortunately, this deficiency tends to be exaggerated to an extreme, often because his unrealistic expectations make him incapable of self-approval. This is particularly true of the perfectionist individual, who is never fully pleased with his accomplishments.

One of my sons is an excellent pianist. In the ninth grade he played his first piano solo in our evening church service; I was elated with his performance and, needless to say, quite proud of him. After the service I gave him a bear hug and exclaimed, "Lee, you played superbly tonight!" He didn't crack a smile. "No, I didn't," he replied; "I missed a note!" Failure to him was one bad note out of 500. It all depends upon your frame of reference.

"I get so disgusted with myself" or "I'll never amount to anything" are typical cries of the depressed. This temperament-induced tendency is so important that we will devote an entire chapter to it later.

(3) *Unfair comparisons*—Every time you compare yourself with someone who scores more favorably than you, depression may ensue. Discontent with what you have and are will direct your thoughts inward and generate depression. Most of the time, of course, you pursue an unfair comparison, matching an area of your deficiency against that of someone else's strength. What makes the comparison particularly ill-advised is that you are not cognizant of the other person's weaknesses,

and thus your envy fastens your interest almost exclusively on your discontent.

Comparisons involving material possessions are especially dangerous. King David of Israel wisely admitted, "I was envious . . . when I saw the prosperity of the wicked" (Ps. 73:3). We may understandably crave a friend's personal warmth or sense of humor, but we must not envy his possessions, popularity, talents, or looks. The wise man heeds the admonition, ". . . be content with such things as ye have" (Heb. 13:5).

(4) *Ambivalence*—Some psychiatrists, like Dr. Ostow, consider ambivalence "the most common precipitative cause of depression." He defines ambivalence as ". . . the sense of being trapped, that is, being unable to remedy an intolerable situation."[1] The individual may shift into ambivalence in his mental attempt to escape his present situation, adopting a position between love and hate—an attitude of indifference.

Feeling trapped is not only one of the causes of depression, but a major reason for divorce. If a couple, for instance, is forced by an unwanted pregnancy to get married, the young husband or mother may feel ensnared, and a period of ambivalence may eventually erupt into anger. Many couples who experience no such trauma at their wedding still feel "trapped." Having several children early in the marriage, lacking proper vocational skills, or enduring heavy weights of responsibility may create an ambivalent depression which develops into an increasing animosity toward anyone who, according to their perspective, devised the trap. In marriage, of course, this is the partner. In adolescence the parent bears the brunt of the young person's wrath when he is "trapped" by school, authority, or responsibility.

The capable career woman who is confined to the home with pre-school children commonly feels trapped. Her situation becomes particularly difficult if she is experienced in the business world and thoroughly enjoys

---

[1] *Ibid.,* p. 82.

that challenge. Because housework, diapers, and baby talk do not stimulate her, she may feel trapped by the very people she loves most.

The modern emphasis on women's lib and career-ism for women will seriously compound this problem. When I asked one woman, "What do you do?" she replied rather sadly, "Oh, I'm just a housewife and mother!" With this attitude growing rapidly today, we can expect depression to increase. Actually, when considered in the light of one's lifetime, what could be better than being a "housewife and mother," or a husband and father? Faulty mental values inevitably lead to depression.

(5) *Sickness*—Everyone has his breaking point. We have already seen that some people can endure more pressure or depression-producing circumstances than others. But whatever your tolerance level for depression it will be lowered through illness. Protracted periods of illness make you even more vulnerable, and the side effects of some drugs may amplify the problem. Dr. Ostow explains this dilemma at great length.

"Some of the factors which can trigger depression are entirely organic. For example, individuals who have had infectious hepatitis are apt to discover that despite good physical recovery, they are left with a profound enervation which leaves them not only inert, but often depressed. Infectious mononucleosis has a similar though perhaps less pronounced tendency to favor depression. We have already noted, in the previous chapter, that the brain disorder called parkinsonism usually includes depression as one of its component elements. Drugs may have a depressing effect too. For example, the drug called reserpine is often prescribed for high blood pressure. It is effective in lowering blood pressure but, in susceptible individuals, it may precipitate clinical depression. Because of this depressing tendency, it functions as a true tranquilizer and can be used in the treatment of schizophrenia, for example. Other true tranquilizers, when administered for one purpose or another, may also precipitate depression. Cortisone and similar steroid drugs often make an individual seem more energetic and livelier. However, given in large enough doses and over long enough periods of time, these drugs may precipitate depression. It has been reported by a number of physicians that regular use of oral contraceptive drugs tends to facilitate depression. This claim has not been substantiated but, on the other hand, it cannot be dismissed."[2]

In addition, when a person is weakened or debilitated by illness, things that would ordinarily not bother him tend to be unduly magnified. It is probably easier to drift into self-pity during an illness than at any other time.

(6) *Biological malfunction*—Many authorities attribute a sizable number of depressions to biological or glandular malfunctions. Abnormal thyroid is often one of the first things considered; others dispute this claim, asserting that depression is brought on by an improper reaction to some traumatic experience. Those holding this view insist that only in rare instances is depression caused biologically. It is not difficult to find experts representing both positions.

Because some depressed people have responded to medication, it is assumed that their problem was due to an abnormal body function. Some have even suggested a disorder in the chemistry of the brain. A doctor friend of mine indicated that a great deal of research is being developed in this area, and consequently it is too early to be dogmatic. Even if biological malfunctions associated with the depression can be established, these findings will not prove whether or not the malfunction was spontaneous or brought on by a faulty thinking pattern. Because a negative or self-destroying thinking pattern can induce harmful changes in the operation of the body and thus adversely affect the body's delicate chemistry and hormonal balance, seriously depressed people should see their doctor. By following his medical suggestions and by using the thinking patterns offered by this book, even those whose depression may be attributed to physical problems can be helped.

---

[2]*Ibid.*, p. 72, 73.

(7) *Postpartum depression*—Practically every book on depression available today includes the problem of postpartum depression. Even a sanguine young mother may experience depression shortly after the birth of her child, quite often because of the emotional exhaustion that follows childbirth. In varying degrees the mother is conscious for nine months that a new life is growing within her. Suddenly she is empty, and in addition she is pressed quickly into a new way of life. It should be of comfort to such a victim to know that the letdown feeling or exhaustion is quite normal and soon passes. One added word of warning in this regard: a mother may escape this experience after her first child but encounter it with her second or third.

Fantasies and illusions never seem to be as good as the real thing. Within a couple of days the new mother discovers that babies are not "cuddly little things" and soft bundles of love, but noisy, fussy, smelly, demanding creatures. She may even resent nursing the child if the process becomes painful. Her depression may cause her to feel guilty and inadequate, which in turn will protract her dilemma.

The best medicine I know for postpartum depression is tender loving care from the baby's father. If he is a mature young man and loves his wife more than himself, he will shower his emotionally spent wife with patience, kindness and affection. She may be irritable, unreasonable and difficult to live with at this time, perhaps even hard to love, but the husband must remember he contributed to her condition and should now seek to boost her morale and self-confidence. For this reason I usually urge the young father to take a week of vacation when the baby is born and give himself to caring for his wife. Such a love investment reaps wonderful dividends in the future. Many women who tend to resent their husband's solicitation the first week or two later come to appreciate it after the depression passes. As one woman admitted, "I treated him like a dog right after the baby was born, but later I came to realize what a wonderful man he was."

Occasionally this period of depression lingers on

too long. Until better medical evidence to the contrary becomes available, I am suspicious that the mother's thinking pattern is the problem. If, for example, ample time for her vitality and energy to return has passed but her depression has not departed, she is probably indulging in self-pitying thoughts. Many women who turned out to be wonderful mothers have confessed that for a long period after the birth of their child they resented the child. They chafed at the constant drain on their energy, nerves, and time. They were even irritated at having to share the affections of their husband or the limelight with their friends.

Believe it or not, some women enjoy being pregnant! I shared that with a mother of six who retorted, "You must be kidding!" No, some women relish the attention they receive when "great with child." However, after delivery the baby gets all the attention. Some depressed-prone women, driven by a feeling of emptiness, delight in the "full" feeling they experience during pregnancy but are engulfed with an empty feeling after childbirth. Such women create severe difficulties for themselves because of their faulty thinking patterns.

(8) *Hyper mental activity*—The active, productive person occasionally encounters a rather strange form of depression during the fifth or sixth decade of life. Not prone to depression by nature, he experiences great difficulty in coping with it. Not much has been written on the subject, but in recent years it has been increasingly under study. By the time the activity-prone, choleric individual reaches the fifth or sixth decade of life, his life style is so cluttered with detail, promotion, and energy that it is difficult for him to rest mentally. Thoughts seem to short-circuit one another, and for the first time his powers of concentration begin to fail. This is an unnerving experience for a usually secure person. Reacting with annoyance and frustration because he cannot sustain his focus on an important matter, he fails to realize that the more he fusses at himself and anticipates the problem, the longer it will persist. If he does not learn efficient methods of managing his time

and personal affairs, he is apt to continue this short-circuiting with increasing severity.

An apparent symptom of this form of depression is sudden irritability for no obvious reason. One father, arriving home from work to a house he enjoyed and to children he loved, suddenly became aware of the teen-age hubbub and jangling. Responding with hostility and rage, he spoke sharply to the children and then hurried to his bedroom to reflect upon his unusual behavior. "What's wrong with me?" he wondered. "The children have acted this way for years. Why should I respond so harshly now?"

Some doctors feel that the problem is caused by a hormonal or chemical change in the system, which is quite possible. Yet unresolved is whether the intense mental activity of the person gives inadequate rest to the brain, causing it to react this way and in turn establishing a chain reaction in the glands, all of which could create the hormonal or chemical imbalance. In any case, such depression usually responds well to medication. One doctor has put more than 500 such patients on a mild form of dilanten, which he feels is the best means of treatment. In fact, he acknowledged that he himself was taking the medication and approved its results. Some doctors prescribe a form of tranquilizer to reverse the activity syndrome immediately and then suggest a reduction in work schedule and an emphasis on leisure activity as a further means of remedy. Most activity-prone people, however, tend to prefer the medication so as to maintain their increased workload.

(9) *Rejection*—At the risk of becoming unduly repetitive, I would like to reassert the tremendous love need in every human being. When that need goes unfulfilled, depression is the escape hatch people use to cope with it. Such depression begins early for the unwanted child who fears rejection by his parents. It occurs among the adolescent who feels rejected by his peer group, the wife who senses the rejection of her husband or woman she admires. Men share the experience when they forfeit the affection of their wife, lose

their job, or suffer the betrayal of a trusted friend. Many times the depression is out of proportion to the rejection, especially when the individual concentrates on the injustice of the rejection and his subsequent loneliness.

(10) *Inadequate goals*—In my chapter on depression in *Spirit-Controlled Temperament*, I wrote, "There is a natural psychological letdown whenever a great project has been completed." Eight years have passed since I wrote that, and I am now inclined to feel that the problem is really one of inadequate goals.

Man is clearly a goal-striving creature. Without goals he ceases to struggle, but whenever we let a project become our primary goal, we inevitably experience a letdown after its attainment. For that reason everyone should maintain long-range as well as short-range goals, and he should frequently upgrade his goals. Extremely goal-conscious people are rarely depressed. Prior to finishing one project, they originate three others! We could all learn a lesson from them: never indulge a mental vacuum. Instead, cultivate the art of setting goals.

One self-pitying woman used to wail, "I have nothing to look forward to." Obviously she was spending too much time thinking about herself. A world so filled with moody, problem-laden people documents the fact that too many individuals lack worthwhile goals.

## Worthwhile Goals

Never settle for second-rate or selfish goals. Earl Nightingale, who probably has helped to motivate more people than any other living person, advises that people desiring success should never try to get rich. Above all, set goals for yourself that involve helping other people; the riches will follow. He has certainly captured the biblical principle, "Give and it shall be given unto you." The richest people I know are those who have given themselves unselfishly to other people. Such motivation will affect the way you sell, cook, teach, or ply your particular trade. True riches, of course, are totally unrelated to money or material reward. In fact, if a person has earned money without helping people, his money will not buy him happiness.

A perceptive real-estate friend who sold rather expensive homes observed that a big house never brought happiness. But if the people bought a big home with money they earned helping other people, they tended to enjoy that home. He expressed his homespun philosophy in these words, "Instead of being a status symbol, a home should be an expression of how much help a person has been to his fellowman." Of one thing I am sure: happy people have strong goals—and somehow these include helping other people. They can also be assured that they will never run out of people to help.

## Summary

Depression does not just happen. It always has a cause. Even in the case of postpartum depression, when there seems to be no explainable cause, the birth of the child triggers it. As basic and common as these ten causes are, they do not *really* comprise the true causes of depression, for many people have faced all these problems without being depressed. Why is it that some people escape the problem while others are engulfed by it? Actually, some of these *causes of* depression are not causes at all but are *excuses for* depression. These causes are to depression what meringue is to a pie. It looks good and tastes good, but meringue is no substitute for pie. These reasons, then, are merely the covering for the real problem, which will be analyzed in the next three chapters.

# 6

# Is There a Cure for Depression?

For at least 2500 years man has made serious attempts to cure depression. In recent times medical science and motivational studies of the mechanism of the human mind have produced rather significant attempts to remedy the problem, but whether these cures are really valid is a matter of controversy among equally competent experts.

The three most popular attempts to cure depression today are drug therapy, electrotherapy, and psychotherapy. Each method has its loyal devotees, and some analysts use combinations of two or three of them. We shall look at each of them in turn and, in addition, consider the one I believe is even more successful—spiritual therapy. It should be kept in mind that the treatment for depression depends upon the cause of the depression, the resources of the one to whom the depressed person has gone for help, and the depth of the depression.

## Drug Therapy

Drugs have been utilized in an attempt to help depressed people since the beginning of recorded history. "More than 2000 years ago Hippocrates prescribed hellebore for the emotionally ill."[1] Before that the Chinese used ephedrine for nervous disorders. Medical literature also reports that in many of the older civilizations opiates, herbs, and other plant and berry extracts were selected for their sedative effects. Interestingly enough, the medicine men of primitive cultures used extracts of cocoa leaves, peyote root and poppy seed for their hallucinogenic effects in counteracting the pain or lethargy of anxiety or depressive states. Far more sophisticated, chemically manufactured drugs are produced today by pharmaceutical houses as the result of painstaking research and experimentation. Most of the drugs currently prescribed by doctors have been introduced into the market since 1955. Dr. Mortimer Ostow, New York neurologist and psychiatrist, has this to say about drug therapy. "In the past decade or so we have acquired a new weapon in the treatment of depressive illness, namely antidepressant drugs. These drugs are not actually antagonists to the psychologic processes associated with depression, but only to the depletion of psychic energies. Antidepressant drugs may be considered to be psychic energizers. After the depression has been reversed by the drug, however, the ambivalence in the anaclitic object relation continues but it can no longer enforce energy depletion or deficiency.

"We can list the following among the advantages of drug treatment. . . . It can be used even in patients too miserable to cooperate in psychotherapy. . . . The patient usually obtains relief after about four to six weeks of daily medication. (It has been recently observed that by administering the drugs by injection for the first few days, one may obtain a therapeutic result within days rather than weeks.) Drug treatment can be continued, so far as we know, indefinitely. Compared to psychotherapy it is quite inexpensive. It can be used for the treatment of large numbers of patients for whom psychotherapy is not available. After some experience, general practitioners and internists learn to

---

[1] Leonard Cammer, *Up From Depression* (New York: Simon and Schuster, 1971), p. 133.

use these drugs and are therefore able to care for their depressed patients without referring them to psychiatrists.

"Among the disadvantages of drug therapy we can list the following. It does nothing to remedy the patient's difficulty in object relations. It does nothing to repair family relations. It gives the patient a false sense that his problems have been solved and sometimes that he is even 'supernormal.' Therefore it frequently discourages patients from undertaking psychotherapy which most of them urgently require. Drugs have some side effects which may be distressing and which may make treatment impossible, and a few drugs have some serious toxicity. Perhaps fifteen or twenty percent of patients do not respond to drug therapy. If object relations continue to deteriorate and to generate a greater and greater degree of ambivalence, the ambivalence may overcome the effect of the drug and the patient may relapse. Since depletion of psychic energy protects against psychotic detachment, the administration of energizing drugs may precipitate schizophrenic psychosis.

"The antidepressant drugs, evidently, do not offer the ideal solution to depression. Since they require four weeks or more before they become effective when given orally, they leave the patient exposed to suicide risk for at least that period of time. The effective dose cannot be ascertained in advance. Therefore the doctor must choose between starting with a small dose and gradually increasing it in order to prevent side effects, and starting with a good dose to speed the effect and thereby risking distressing side effects. Sometimes the side effects can be so distressing that the patient will resist taking the drug."[2]

Recently a woman informed me that she had found her husband's diet pills to be the perfect solution to her depression. She did not realize, however, that those diet pills were probably a form of amphetamine which was never intended for permanent use, but for short

---

[2]Ostow, pp. 114, 115.

periods to help in food intake reduction. In addition to cutting down on one's appetite, they also stimulated the "pleasure center" of the brain just above the hypothalamus gland, producing a feeling of euphoria in direct proportion to the amount of amphetamine taken and the user's natural immunity level.

They trouble with amphetamines is that they become addictive—even dangerously so. In fact, they are one of the more easily obtained drugs that are largely responsible for the increase in drug abuse during the past decade. The body's natural immunity level responds to this drug, making it necessary to increase the dosage to continue the same effects. In addition, the exhilarating "high" that amphetamines produce is followed by a corresponding "low" which, not surprisingly, sends the individual into a worse depression than before he began to take the drug. The woman mentioned above, like scores of others, compounded her problems by taking her husband's pills. Not only did she feel worse after taking his "diet pills," but her husband was upset that his pills had disappeared. I have repeatedly observed that people on diet pills are usually irritable and tend, like this woman, to aggravate a bad situation. Her first visit concerned an emotional problem. After taking the amphetamines she added a marital problem.

Dr. Leonard Cammer, another psychiatrist, favors electrotherapy and is somewhat critical of drug therapy. In his book *Up From Depression* he states, "No drug will always do exactly and only what is asked of it for everyone. An aspirin may relieve a headache in one case. In another, it can irritate the stomach and induce heartburn; or it can also cause ringing in the ears. The latter two symptoms are side effects.

"Antidepressants, tranquilizers, and stimulant drugs, all powerful and complex chemicals, can give rise to quite a few side effects in different people or in the same person at different times. Most of them are not serious. For example, an antidepressant may cause the person to perspire and develop dryness of the mouth, mild constipation, and some blurring of vision. While these side effects can be distinctly annoying, they are not critical.

"But what if the person's special sensitivity to the drug produces side effects that signal more than this? Perhaps danger? While the incidence of such sensitivities remains small they can occur. For example, some drugs may raise or lower the blood pressure when combined with alcohol, certain foods, or other medication. Still others can destroy blood corpuscles and leave the person open to infection, liver trouble, or other complications. To be sure, none of this need go to serious proportions if your relative, when placed on a drug program for depression, remains under medical care and observation."[3]

Dr. Cammer further reports that only thirty-five percent of those with acute depressions were cured by drugs.[4] Most of the reports I have read indicate that drug therapy is not nearly as successful as the medical layman is apt to think.

## Electrotherapy

During the forties and fifties the most prominent method of treating depression involved electric-shock treatments. Dr. Mortimer Ostow, who seems to favor drug therapy, notes, "Until the advent of antidepressant drugs, the only organic treatment for melancholic depression was the procedure we call electric-shock therapy. In this treatment a brief electric shock is administered to the brain, and it produces an instantaneous convulsion and leaves a temporary amnesia. As it is ordinarily administered, these treatments are repeated about three times a week until a total of five, ten, or twenty treatments is administered. As the treatments continue, the amnesia becomes more and more intense. The energizing drugs have replaced electric-

---

[3]Cammer, p. 137.
[4]*Ibid.*, p. 139.

shock treatment to a large extent, though the replacement is more complete in some institutions than in others."[5]

It is obvious from the above quotation that Dr. Ostow does not regard electric-shock treatment as the best method in use today for treating depression. Others, apparently just as well qualified, are much more favorable toward the practice. Consider Dr. Cammer's enthusiastic appraisal.

"An abundance of recorded evidence and validated experience has shown that EST, in accordance with recognized medical standards, is considered to be a safe procedure. This is especially true when it is given by a trained and competent psychiatrist who can evaluate his patient's condition and is prepared to deal with any expected contingency that may arise during the treatment. I, along with many other psychiatrists, prefer to be assisted by an anesthesiologist. In my opinion, this further insures an uneventful recovery from the treatment."[6]

To a medical layman electric-shock treatments seem quite frightening. For that reason, in an attempt to be fair, I will extend Dr. Cammer's favorable presentation in order to specify the means whereby treatment is administered.

"Treatments can be administered at any time of the day, provided that the patient has not eaten for four hours or more.

"He or she reclines on a comfortable bed. In a doctor's office, ordinary street clothes are worn, but these are loosened. The shoes are removed.

"Then a quick-acting barbiturate is injected intravenously; this puts the patient to sleep in about ten seconds. From this point on, the patient feels nothing and remains asleep until after the treatment. (While most persons do not like to contemplate being 'put out,' many patients tell me that they welcome the pleasant sensation of falling asleep quickly and smoothly, possi-

---

[5]Ostow, p. 117.
[6]Cammer, p. 152.

bly because they experience an instant release from mental pain.)

"Following the sleep-inducing injection a second chemical, succinylcholine (*suk*-sin-ill-*ko*-leen) is administered. This drug is a relaxant which eliminates all strong muscular contractions. It takes about twenty to thirty seconds for the muscles to relax sufficiently for purposes of treatment.

"Now the patient breathes pure oxygen by positive pressure through a face mask. This ensures full oxygenation of all body tissues. At the same time, an extremely low-amperage electric current, applied to the temples for one second or less, provides the stimulus for the neural discharge that will set the healing process in motion.

"The patient sleeps throughout this procedure.

"The entire treatment is painless except for the pinprick of the first injection. In all it has taken about two minutes.

"Now for the initial recovery phase, which extends over ten to fifteen minutes but sometimes less: in the first minutes or so, the anesthetic wears off and the effects of the muscle relaxant lift. Then (in about ten minutes) the after-discharge and deep sleep of the electric stimulation pass into light sleep.

"After an additional ten to twenty minutes the patient awakens but feels a bit groggy. Soon the whereabouts and the identities of those in the surroundings are recognized. The patient is then allowed to sit up. Gradually, the fuzzy feeling clears and orientation is regained. *At no time does he or she remember the treatment.*

"The entire procedure from start to finish has taken about one hour. The patient can now go home. If the treatment was given in a hospital he returns to his room."[7]

The two major complaints of electric-shock patients is that they experience a loss of memory and fear that the process might be harmful to the brain. Dr.

---

[7] *Ibid.*, pp. 151, 152.

Cammer attempts to cancel these fears by assuring us, "I have found no convincing clinical or research evidence to confirm that EST impairs the brain. After extensive use throughout the world for over thirty years it is plain that in a large majority of cases EST *benefits* the person. By means of it he or she becomes rational and well. But if you put it this way—does EST *alter* brain function?—yes. When the brain is stimulated by electricity or chemicals in the dosages required and the duration called for, the treatment clearly modifies brain activity toward improvement. Indeed, it is given *in order to create responses that are part of this modification.*

"If there are any permanent side effects on brain tissue as a result of EST, these cannot be demonstrated by any reliable tests. To me it is apparent that electric and chemical application to the brain produces stimulatory effects that help the depressed person return to normal function."[8]

Currently, an increasing number of doctors are becoming disenchanted with EST. Dr. Cammer, however, indicates that it is still used "to a great extent, despite the current vogue for drug treatment and the case with which drugs are provided. Indeed, because the advent of drugs has also brought with it many serious complications, we have seen a widespread return to EST, as the safer, more reliable, and effective method for treating disabling depressions. The clinical evidence is conclusive: compared with the thirty-five percent statistic for recovery with drugs, EST gets seventy to eighty percent of persons with endogenous depressions well—doing twice as good a job as the drugs. In reactive and neurotic depressions, the overall improvement rates with EST are about the same as with drug treatment, except in their very severe manifestations, when EST produces a more clear-cut remission in a much shorter period of time."[9] All doctors do not share his enthusiasm for EST because those I polled indi-

[8]*Ibid.,* p. 154.
[9]*Ibid.,* pp. 159, 160.

cated they only recommend EST as a last resort, and none was convinced it was really successful seventy to eighty percent of the time.

## Shock Therapy Out

Dr. Ronald Fieve, Chief of Psychiatric Research at the New York State Psychiatric Institute, thinks the new drug "Lithium Carbonate" has made electric-shock therapy and most other drug therapies obsolete. In a report to the 122nd Annual Convention of The American Medical Association, he said, "There is no longer the same need for using electro-shock therapy, except in a small number of acutely assaultive manic or suicidal patients, and many physicians have yet to catch up with this idea and needlessly continue using electro-shock or multiple drug therapies."[10] Thus the battle rages in the medical profession concerning the best method for dealing with the depressed. It is obvious that equally competent men have differing opinions.

As a non-medical counselor it has been my observation that electric-shock therapy, like drug therapy, will provide only minimal success unless one of two things occurs. Either there is a change in the circumstances that caused the depression, or the patient experiences a change of the thinking pattern that induced it; otherwise, in spite of the therapy used, the depression will recur in time.

One of my counselees had shock treatments on two separate occasions separated by a five-year interval. Apparently feeling a retrogression, she came in for help. After analyzing the problem, we found that the shock treatments had only cured the symptoms, not the problem that caused them. Consequently there was a recurring need for more treatments. Her difficulty was one of intense guilt. When her guilt consciousness was removed, then indeed she was capable of a normal happy life. It never became necessary for her to undergo the third set of treatments.

[10]"New Drug Helps Manic Patients," *San Diego Union*, June 22, 1973, p. A8.

## Psychotherapy

Even before the days of Sigmund Freud, psychotherapy was the most common method of treating the depressed. In fact, it was used almost exclusively until EST came into view during the 1940s. Simply defined, psychotherapy is "talk treatment." It consists of a depressed patient speaking freely to a counselor. Because the counselee is depressed due to a faulty thinking pattern, the counselor must examine his values and judgments toward other people so as to help him understand himself better and learn how to relate properly to others.

Since a high percentage of depression is kindled by the rejection or loss of a love object, a warm and empathetic counselor can frequently provide the counselee with an adequate substitute. Probably the most therapeutic part of psychotherapy is that the despairing individual who feels rejected, hopeless, and alone has access to the patience, understanding, and concern of a counselor. If the counselor can sufficiently supply his patient's needs, counseling can often provide a very meaningful crutch upon which the depressed person may lean.

Significant drawbacks to psychotherapy include its painstakingly long and exceptionally expensive process. Most people cannot afford a lengthy series of counseling sessions from $30 to $50 an hour. The non-directive counselor believes that he should never impose his perspective or concepts on the individual, but merely serve as a sounding board to the counselee, who should organize his own principles for living. Psychotherapy often becomes an exercise in futility because it assumes that the solution to the counselee's problem lies deep within the patient and the counselor's task is simply to help draw it forth. Usually the individual does *not* have the answer within himself. Frequently protracted sessions of non-directive counseling may result in frustration for both the counselor and the counselee.

Psychotherapy may become dangerous when a counselor seeks to impose his principles upon the counselee, who is soliciting help because of his desperate condition. If the counselor is an amoral individual and finds that the counselee has serious guilt problems that cause his depression, he may try to explain away the patient's guilt and accordingly deny his moral principles. I have observed the result when an individual's moral values were ridiculed and attacked, and he was encouraged to pursue a loose, amoral pattern of living. When such advice comes from a professionally trained psychiatrist, it may sound quite convincing. Unfortunately, the new style of immoral behavior usually brings a short period of exhilaration but in many cases is followed eventually by an overwhelming consciousness of guilt that far exceeds the original problem.

Several years ago I read an article by a psychiatrist who was critical of his own profession. He stated that he had observed fifty to seventy percent of the depressed people who consulted a psychiatrist being helped during a two-year period. In addition he noted that fifty to seventy percent of those who consulted a minister, medical doctor, or good friend gained relief. But he was particularly disturbed in that fifty to seventy percent of those who received no aid whatsoever improved over a two-year period.

This does not suggest that depressed people do not need help. But many of us who have been counseling people for twenty-five years and more are not convinced that psychotherapy has the answer. In fact, some of the results of group therapy, sensitivity therapy and other humanistic fads now being propagated can be downright dangerous.

One thirty-year-old single woman's depression drove her to psychotherapy. Her "Victorian ideas" were so blasted during group therapy that she later submitted to intercourse with four different men within two weeks. When she came into my office, she was not only depressed but staggering under an overwhelming load of guilt. In addition, she was pregnant. For this kind of treatment she should pay $75.00? There must be a better way!

## Man Has a Spiritual Side to His Nature

The form of therapy most commonly neglected by secular doctors, psychiatrists, and counselors today is spiritual therapy. Because our educational system is overwhelmingly secularized and based on atheistic humanism, little or no consideration is given to the highly significant spiritual side of man's nature. The secular view of man as body, mind, and emotions is *completely inadequate,* and man will never solve the problems of man on a permanent basis until he recognizes that void. Man is an intensely spiritual being, which distinguishes him from the animal kingdom. Unless therapy includes a remedy for his spiritual nature, it will offer only minimal or temporary results.

All forms of therapy agree on one principle: a depressed person must be aided externally. Whether involving electric shock or a counselor, all current therapy involves something or someone outside of the individual to support and sustain him. Those of us who utilize spiritual therapy in our counseling technique similarly acknowledge the need for this external power, for we have found it to be a forceful tool in reaching the total person.

The following diagram illustrates the four distinct parts of the total person. No man is complete without all of them. No man can function to the maximum without all of them. We are all aware of the mental, emotional, and physical, but few realize the tremendous importance of the spiritual dimension.

One of the great tragedies of our times is that atheistic humanists have so brainwashed our culture into thinking man is an animal without a spiritual dimension to life that most people possess few spiritual reserves upon which to draw in times of mental, emotional, or physical distress. Instead, the giant God-void within them seriously compounds their problems and hampers recovery.

THE FOUR PARTS OF MAN

To illustrate the power of spiritual therapy to change a person's life, we shall consider briefly the other three sides of man's nature.

(1) *Physical*—Everyone is conscious of the physical aspect of life, the part of our being on which we spend tens of thousands of dollars during a lifetime. In truth, it is the least important part, for unless the other three parts of our nature function properly, our body will malfunction. As we shall see, our physical body is controlled by our emotions.

(2) *Emotional*—Of the three parts of man's nature that are widely accepted today, the least understood is the emotional. Everyone is sensitive to love and hate, and we have all heard of "the heart," particularly on Valentine's Day. The heart, or seat of the emotions,

is not located in the physical heart, of course, but between one's temples slightly behind the forehead. Scientists call this the emotional center of man. This emotional switchboard seems to work electronically in conjunction with every organ of the body. Before any bodily movement takes place, it must first be electronically notified by the emotional center. Consequently, the condition of this center will affect the condition of the entire body. If a person is emotionally at peace, his body will function normally. If his heart or emotional center is upset, he will feel the effects throughout his body.

We are all familiar with the term "emotionally induced illness." Doctors today indicate that seventy to eighty-five percent of all physical ailments are provoked by emotional disturbance. Such debilitating diseases as heart trouble, high blood pressure, ulcers, asthma, and some forms of arthritis derive from emotional tension. Dr. S. I. McMillan in his excellent book *None of These Diseases* states that there are fifty-one emotionally induced diseases. That is why a depressed person usually feels sickly if he indulges his depression for a protracted period.

Emotions are not generated spontaneously. Our emotions flow from the thinking pattern of the mind. Suppose, for example, that you are spontaneously asked to come to the platform and address a large audience. If you are not trained for that kind of experience, your mind will immediately set up self-conscious thought patterns producing fear or fright, which in turn will effect a physiological change in your body. Your uneasiness will occasion knocking knees and restricted saliva glands. Your normal voice may be completely restricted, creating a high or screechy sound. Thus emotional tension, fashioning a rapid chain reaction, affects the entire body.

Another common illustration relates to worry. Whenever our minds are confronted with such problems as unpaid bills or indefinite circumstances, we begin to worry. Emotional tension protracted over a long period can bring about a physical breakdown or sickness.

Since man's emotions control his body, we must examine what controls our emotions—the mind.

(3) *Mental*—The mind is a phenomenal tabulating mechanism. Some have designated it "the most complicated computer in the world." The memory capability of the human mind is almost beyond belief. There are strong indications that the subconscious mind retains every thought, every sight, and every sound. When hypnotists have regressed their subjects back to the early days of infancy, amazingly accurate details of their life are revealed. The best estimates today suggest that only a very few people use more than ten percent of their mental potential.

The mind is composed of the conscious and the subconscious. Although the subconscious mind cannot be controlled, as we shall show in a later chapter, it is highly responsive to visual suggestion. "You are what you think!" accurately conveys the situation, for thinking incites our feelings. Whatever we put in our minds causes responses in our emotional center, which in turn activates a physical response. Note the symbols shown in the chart below. Follow the arrows to comprehend how powerfully the mind influences the emotions and body. The five senses are the windows to the mind, particularly the eyes and ears. Be sure of this: whatever you put into your mind through your eyes or ears initiates a response in your heart and in turn motivates the body.

We may clearly illustrate this principle with the effects of pornographic literature. The reading of such literature will fan the passions which motivate and prepare your body to sexual action. By contrast, if you read clean, wholesome literature, you will enrich your emotions, producing wholesome desires and motivations in the body.

Every young man whom I have counseled concerning sex problems has acknowledged that he had been aroused repeatedly by sexually inflammatory material or viewing suggestive or X-rated movies. His drives were not spontaneous, but clearly traceable to his reading or viewing matter.

THE FOUR PARTS OF MAN

The same can be said for violent action. Long before a person erupts into an angry response, he has seen, heard, or thought about those things that produced the emotions of hate which finally were put into motion. That is why Christ said, "Whosoever hateth his brother has committed murder already in his heart." No physical murder can exist without emotional murder, and the mind is responsible for the entire sequence.

As we shall see, depression (an emotion) produces apathy physically. Since feelings are caused by the mind, depression must be initiated by a mental thought pattern. Instead of treating the results or symptoms (apathy, sleeplessness, etc.) with drugs or working on the emotions by substitute love objects, counselors, or drugs, we may confer lifelong relief only through a change in one's thinking pattern.

The mind is the problem! But how does one control the uncontrollable mind?

## Spiritual Therapy

Although a few people possess sufficient strength of mind to reverse negative or harmful thinking patterns in order to produce good emotional feelings, which in turn occasion normal body function, they are very scarce. Most people require external help in this area. By voiding his spiritual nature, as secular man is prone to do, he makes himself a slave to his own mental weakness. Most of the people who come to me as a counselor have tried drugs, electrotherapy, or psychotherapy, with negative or minimal results. In my opinion such persons can be helped only by availing themselves of spiritual therapy.

A professional boxer would never enter the ring with a black patch over one eye and one arm tied behind his back. Such a sight, nevertheless, graphically illustrates the dilemma secular man finds himself in today. By neglecting the spiritual side of his nature, he has blinded himself to the tremendous power available to him in overcoming depression, fear, anger, and other detrimental emotional maladies.

His problem is further compounded by the God-void in his life created by spiritual neglect. Pascal, the great French philosopher, once said, "There is a God-shaped vacuum in the heart of every man that can be satisfied by none other save God himself." That God-shaped vacuum keeps man on a treadmill of restless activity and propels him on a constant quest for identity and peace. It is impossible to achieve contentment on a lasting basis through the mind, the heart, or the body!

## The Fact of Man's Spiritual Nature

Evidence that man is an intensely spiritual creature is not difficult to obtain. Of all living creatures, only man undertakes a universal quest for God. Man alone reflects a natural built-in religious instinct and universal guilt consciousness.

In my travels around the world, I have made a special effort to examine the archaeological ruins of ancient civilizations. Before long I began to recognize that the oldest of man's buildings were temples, shrines, or houses of religious worship, indicating man's universal religious hunger. What produces that hunger? It is his natural God-given spiritual instinct or nature.

Even communist leaders, who brand religion as the "opiate of the people," have had to wrestle with the fact that man is "incurably religious." This universal religious quest of mankind must have a discernible cause. Just as man experiences the physical needs of hunger and thirst, emotional needs such as love, and mental needs as evidenced by curiosity, so he has deep spiritual needs, manifested by his quest for God.

Some of the most hardened atheists have been found to demonstrate their spiritual instinct at the moment of death. We have all heard of prayerless individuals who lived totally unconscious of God during their lives, in some cases even antagonistic to Him, but when the specter of death was thrust upon them, they called for God. When I was a boy, a notorious community atheist, a bricklayer by profession, fell down a chimney he was erecting. After many unsuccessful attempts were made to extricate him, other bricklayers were summoned to take the chimney apart, brick by brick. Our local newspaper carried the report the next day that when they reached him, they found him praying for deliverance. Rather than attribute this to personal weakness, we must accept it as verification of man's natural spiritual instinct.

Anyone who neglects his spiritual nature does so at his own peril. God has given to man this part of his being to stabilize and motivate his mind, heart, and body. Those who ignore this mighty power station within themselves are like a four-cylinder car functioning on only three cylinders. They do not need new or better spark plugs on the three working cylinders, but full restoration of their inoperative spiritual nature.

## Man's Spiritual Nature

The spiritual side of man's nature contains his will, one of the unique characteristics that distinguishes him from the animal kingdom. God has given to every man a free will. With it he can ignore or reject God, or he can accept and cooperate with Him. Man alone makes that decision but be sure of this: his lasting happiness is dependent upon his choice.

The throne in the spiritual quarter of man's nature symbolizes this free will. The "E" on the throne represents the ego-nature of man, generating the self-conscious or self-oriented man. God gives to every man the opportunity to be master of his own fate, captain of his own soul. The "E" on the throne exhibits ego making his own decisions, independent of God. Such a man is ultimately destined to increasing degrees of frustration and futility in life. The various dots in our diagram represent the many decisions man makes in his lifetime. Every individual must decide such things as where he will live, where he will go to school, and where he will work, what will be his vocation, and whom he will marry. Life is made up of a myriad of decisions, but happiness will untimately be decided by the propriety of man's choices. If he lives self-sufficiently and independent of God, with ego supreme on the throne of his will, he is going to experience varying degrees of frustration, confusion, guilt and fear.

I have shared this diagram with hundreds of people through the years and have yet to find anyone forty years of age or older to argue with me. Recently I shared it with an airline ticket agent as I was returning from a two-week vacation in Hawaii. She indicated that at twenty-two years of age she had everything to live for, but when I turned to her and asked if she felt this frustration and futility in her life, she put her face in her hands and burst into tears. She wept so profusely that the tears flooded from between her fingers. Although more dramatic than most, her experience is not uncommon.

Most miserable or depressed people are not conscious of the fact that their misery emanates from the God-vacuum within them. This spiritual deficiency or God-void makes them vulnerable to a variety of mental, emotional and physical maladies or disorders. Whether they are antagonistic to God or just neglect His presence in their lives seems to make no difference, They experience an empty hunger within them for God, but they lack the spiritual resources to help them cope with the problems caused by their ego-dominated decisions. This God-void is universally as old as man. The Bible calls it "death." In the Garden of Eden when Adam and Eve rebelled and disobeyed God, they died spiritually. That spiritual death has been transmitted from generation to generation, conferring a serious void within the life of every human being. Although man can gain momentary happiness on the mental, emotional, or physical planes of life, he will never attain lasting happiness as long as the God-void in his spiritual nature is unfulfilled. He will never know abiding joy or have power to control those weaker parts of his nature.

## Jesus Christ Fills the God-Void

Jesus Christ is God's special remedy to fill the God-void in every human being. That He lived over 1900 years ago is a matter of historical fact. Why He lived, however, is too often a source of confusion, even though the only authentic record of His life gives us the answer. Jesus Christ Himself said, "I am come that they might have life, and that they might have it more abundantly" (John 10:10). The abundant life He offers not only fills the God-void in a person's spirit, but also provides him with power to eliminate depression and other emotional problems.

A very emotionally burdened man came to Jesus Christ one night (John 3:1-13), inquiring how he might come into a personal relationship with God. Jesus said, "Verily, verily, I say unto thee, Except a man be born again, he cannot see the kingdom of God." Obviously puzzled by Christ's explanation, Nicodemus asked, "How can a man be born when he is old? can he enter the second time into his mother's womb, and be born?" Jesus answered, "Verily, verily, I say unto thee, Except a man be born of water and of the Spirit, he cannot enter into the kingdom of God." The context of this passage clearly indicates that Nicodemus needed a personal spiritual experience. Just as he had been born physically to enter this world, he had to be born spiritually to fulfill his destiny and prepare for the next world. This spiritual birth of power, created by individually receiving Jesus Christ as Lord and Savior, gives a person the external power he needs to cope with his emotional problems. This is particularly true in the case of depression.

Contrary to popular opinion, Jesus Christ is not automatically born within a person; otherwise he would not have need for this spiritual birth. Instead (as illustrated in the next diagram) Jesus Christ is external

MAN WITH CHRIST
IN HIS LIFE

MAN WITHOUT CHRIST
IN HIS LIFE

to man's spiritual nature, for man is born void of God. Through His Holy Spirit and the teaching of the Bible, Christ knocks at the door of man's spiritual consciousness, saying, "If any man hear my voice, and open the door, I will come in to him, and will sup with him, and he with me" (Rev. 3:20). This promise of Christ testifies that any individual conscious of his God-void and rebellion against the will of God can invite Him into his life. Christ never forces His way into an individual's life, but responds only when invited. At that moment, the individual is spiritually made alive. This gives him a consciousness for God and an increased capacity to cope with all the problems of life, including depression.

## Jesus Christ's Explanation

In the Sermon on the Mount, Jesus Christ held forth two pathways to eternity: "the broad road that leads to destruction" and "the narrow road that leads to life." Judged by the increasing number of miserable people today, it is obvious that the majority are on the broad road that leads to destruction—not only eternal destruction, but also mental, emotional, and physical self-destruction. This self-destruction is twofold:

TWO WAYS TO ETERNITY

ETERNAL LIFE

ETERNAL DEATH

(1) leading a life spiritually void of God and (2) reaping the results of decisions made by ego, not by God.

When a person passes the age of accountability and becomes conscious of right and wrong, he proceeds on the broad road that leads to destruction. If his mental, emotional, and physical miseries make him conscious of his spiritual God-void, he may seek divine help. At that point in his life, if he is confronted with the fact that Jesus Christ came into this world to die on the cross for his sins, he can personally receive Him as Lord and Savior.

The greatest expression of love the world has ever known is symbolized by the cross of Jesus Christ. On that cross God's own Son died for the sins of the whole world. Christ, who was God in human flesh and remained sinless during His thirty-three years of life, took on Himself the sins of the whole world and died sacrificially that men through Him might be saved. For that reason He could say, "I am the way, the truth, and the life: no man cometh unto the Father, but by me" (John 14:6). The cross of Christ, then, becomes a bridge upon which men living on the broad road leading to destruction may travel to the wonderful road of life.

## Four Things You Must Realize

To fill the God-void in your life and become spiritually born again, you must realize four things:

(1) Your self-will, rebellion, and sin have separated you from God, creating the God-void within you. You and God alone know the amount of your sin. It may be extensive, it may be moderate; it really doesn't matter. Your sin has separated you from God. You will never know lasting peace and happiness until your sins are forgiven.

(2) Jesus Christ died on the cross that you might be forgiven of your past sins. In God's economy "the wages of sin is death" (Rom. 6:23). However, you do not have to die for yourself or your sins, for Christ has already done this for you.

(3) Jesus Christ rose again that you might be guided and empowered to live the new eternal life. ". . . the gift of God is eternal life through Jesus Christ our Lord." Jesus said, "Because I live, ye shall live also." Christianity in its entirety is built upon the true foundation that Jesus Christ rose from the dead. His personal resurrection three days after His crucifixion is the cornerstone of Christian truth. He not only rose again to give you eternal life in heaven, but the abundant new life here and now. It is this life which will enable you to triumph over your weaknesses.

(4) You must personally receive Him as *Lord* and *Savior* by inviting Him into your life. Since willfulness caused you to be separated from God, increasing the God-void within you, it is imperative that you turn

the controlling force of your life over to Jesus Christ. This must be done by personal invitation. Accepting Him as your Savior and Lord occasions an exchange of roles. When you make Him master of your life, your ego becomes His servant. You still have to make decisions in life, but now your decisions are filtered through Christ. In a practical way it is no longer "What can I do about that?" but "Lord Jesus, what do You wish me to do about that?" No man who lives this latter way will experience a lifetime of misery. Similarly, no man who lives the other way will attain a lifetime of happines.

## The Big Question

Have you ever personally invited Jesus Christ into your life? The best way to answer that question is to ask yourself which of the following two diagrams represents your life right now.

As you deliberate the answer, you should be prepared to pinpoint a time in your life when Jesus Christ was outside and you invited Him in. If there has never been such a time, or you are not sure, I would urge you to bow your head right now and invite Him into your life. If you approach Him sincerely, you have the promise of God that Jesus Christ will come and reside in your life. If you do not know how to pray, I suggest the following prayer:

> Dear God, I admit that I am a sinner and need Jesus Christ in my life to become my Savior and Lord. This day I turn the control of my life over to You. Amen!

## The Promise of God

If you have sincerely uttered that prayer, you have the divine promise of God "that whosoever shall call upon the name of the Lord shall be saved." Let that promise dwell in your mind, because it is the best news you have ever heard. Today you have been "born

FEAR
GUILT
FRUSTRATION
FUTILITY
CONFUSION
DEPRESSION

MAN VOID OF GOD

PARDON    PEACE    POWER
JOY    PURPOSE    CONFIDENCE

MAN WITH GOD

again" (John 3:3-5). You have also been born into the family of God (John 1:12) and guaranteed eternal life.

## The Results of the Christ-Controlled Life

The Christ-controlled life provides a spiritually dynamic power and corresponding assets that are almost beyond comprehension! Let the diagram on page 76 showing man with God burn its way into your mind, and examine each of these key works which signify your inheritance when you accept Christ. The Bible teaches that Jesus Christ has accomplished many things for you, but these six are particularly significant:

(1) *Pardon*—All your sins have been forgiven by the mercy of God through His Son, Jesus Christ. "If we confess our sins, he is faithful and just to forgive us our sins, and to cleanse us from all unrighteousness" (1 John 1:9).

(2) *Peace*—Since your sins are forgiven, you now own the peace of a clear conscience before God. "Therefore being justified by faith, we have peace with God through our Lord Jesus Christ" (Rom. 5:1).

(3) *Power*—A new power will gradually begin to control your life if you walk in the control of the Spirit of Christ. "Therefore if any man be in Christ, he is a new creature: old things are passed away; behold, all things are become new" (2 Cor. 5:17).

(4) *Joy*—Happiness is a transistory experience depending upon external events. Joy is an enduring experience that is contingent upon your relationship to God. As you continue to let Christ control your life, you will experience increasingly protracted periods of joy that often are unrelated to the adversity of your circumstances (Eph. 5:19).

(5) *Purpose*—From the moment you receive Jesus Christ you have a whole new purpose for living. Before becoming a Christian, your purpose was to satisfy yourself. From this day on your purpose is to serve Jesus Christ. The Apostle Paul said it in Acts 9:6, "Lord, what wilt thou have me to do?" That mental

attitude and prayer became the formula for his happy and successful Christian life. Christ said, "Seek ye first the kingdom of God, and his righteousness; and all these things shall be added unto you" (Matt. 6:33). As you seek Him, you will find that He provides adequate strength for every need.

(6) *Confidence*—As you nourish your new spiritual nature by reading, hearing and studying the Bible, you will find an assurance as confidence begins to grow in your life which you have never had before. You as now a child of God! (1 John 5:10-15).

If you sincerely prayed the prayer printed on page 75, you have become a child of God. As such, you enjoy the capacity for living a depressed-free life. That does not guarantee you will, but you do possess the external source of power that will enable you to do so. How to use this power to win over depression is the main purpose of this book.

Although we have devoted an entire chapter to the causes of depression, we purposely reserved the primary causes until this point in the book. Our reason for doing so is very simple. Until an individual has access to the spiritual resources referred to in this chapter, he is incapable of coping with these primary causes of depression. At this point we can proceed not only with a careful consideration of the causes, but also with the remedy that God has made available.

# 7

# The Place of Anger in Depression

Depression always results from a specific cause. That the individual does not know the cause does not eliminate the fact of its existence. In his book *The Psychology of Melancholy,* Dr. Mortimer Ostow says, "Generally, even in the case of individuals who are susceptible to depression, some current insult is needed to trigger the depressive process."[1]

Although we would like to blame depression on organic or psychological changes in the human body, we are forced realistically to admit that it is the result of our reaction to an insult or disappointment or rejection. The first step in the chain reaction producing depression is anger. Don't be surprised that you involuntarily reject such a proposal. I have consistently observed that most depressed persons cannot and do not think of themselves as angry people. A number of individuals with whom I have shared this have challenged me, but on further questioning and closer examination of their thought patterns prior to depression, we established the problem without exception.

Dr. Ostow adds, "Depression, at every phase of its

---

[1]Ostow, p. 72.

development, includes a component of anger, whether visible or invisible, whether conscious or unconscious. This anger is directed against the individual who is expected to provide love but who disappoints. At different phases, the anger may arouse a wish to irritate, to hurt, or to destroy, depending upon the degree of pain which the patient suffers. Even the rebirth fantasy carries a component of anger, for it defiantly asserts that the patient will cure himself and that he does not require the assistance of the 'parent' who disappointed him."[2] Dr. Ostow further explains the problem of anger as follows:

"Some parents regard and treat their children with severe hostility. In these instances the child becomes fixed into a childish pattern in his relation with his parents, and subsequently as an adult is apt to have to contend with a strong depressive tendency. Overt hostility of parent to child seems inhuman and perverse, and yet we know of numbers of such instances. . . . But even currently we read of what is now called the 'battered-child' syndrome. Small children are sometimes brought to the hospital or to the morgue showing signs of severe physical abuse. Investigation discloses that they have been abandoned or actually hurt by their parents. From time to time we read in the newspapers of a child murdered by a parent. . . .

"If we study psychoanalytically patients who harbor hostility toward their children, we find that in each case the parent, as a child, had had to contend with intense anger against his own parent or one of his own siblings; that he had contrived some defensive maneuver to contain that anger, such as reactive affection, loyalty, or subservience to the hated person; and that with the advent of the infant of the new generation the defense had collapsed and the individual was left once more to deal with this overwhelming anger. . . .

"Hostility and rejection by the parent constitute a serious threat to the child. Feeling threatened, he clings more tightly, and this clinging includes both affectionate and hostile components. The intensity of these

---

[2]*Ibid.*, p. 18.

mixed feelings makes the situation traumatic. Traumatic situations tend in general to repeat themselves. The child may respond to any subsequent rejection with aggressive clinging. The child, when he becomes an adult, may attach himself to an unreliable, hostile partner. As an adult, he may provoke rejection by his partner. Or as a parent he may repeat the same pattern with his own child, rejecting the child and abusing it as he was rejected and abused."[3]

The two most powerful human emotions are love and anger. Love is a health-producing emotion, anger a health-destroying emotion. It follows, then, that anger is the most negative and damaging emotion with which man has to cope.

Anger is a natural defense mechanism against insult, rejection, or injury. It explains why many depressed-prone people are angry people or the products of angry homes where they were abused or rejected by their parents. Such anger is not only harmful emotionally, but physically and spiritually as well. I am convinced that the current age of depression is largely caused by the inability of people to cope with their anger. The rebellious, hostile people of the '60s are now becoming the depressed-prone people of the '70s.

The indulgence of children as a result of the false notions of behavioristic psychologists of a past generation has produced a generation of angry, rebellious, hostile, and bitter young people who go from anger to depression. It is not at all uncommon for such individuals when counseled for depression to finally indicate that prior to the depression something had made them angry. It is most helpful for individuals to recognize that depression is not spontaneous, but the result of their anger.

## The High Cost of Anger

It would be impossible to estimate the immense cost of anger emotionally, physically, and spiritually.

---

[3]*Ibid.*, pp. 75, 76, 78, 79.

Emotionally the cost is seen in the needless bitterness it engenders. A recent *Reader's Digest* article explained the tragic deaths of four employees, and the critical wounding of another. The assassin was a "Mr. Niceguy" type, the kind of man who would make a pleasant neighbor. At forty-three years of age he seemingly "went berserk" and shot his fellow employees.

Investigation revealed that his bizarre behavior was not spontaneous. Eighteen months before the tragedy he was bypassed for promotion in favor of someone else. His wife acknowledged that "from that day on he gradually became a different man." It is not difficult to imagine the mental chain reaction he experienced. As he nursed his grudge and indulged his bitterness, mulling over the injustice of the occasion, he became so emotionally distraught that he took his .38 caliber revolver to work and shot five people. One common thread of identity united the victims: they were all in a position to have participated in the matter of his promotion by his company. Today this man is kept behind bars, estranged from the family he loved. Four people met an untimely death, and one may be crippled for life all because of his hostility.

The physical cost of anger produces a tragic toll in human suffering that fills our hospital wards today. The human body can stand only so much stress, and nothing produces tension quite like anger. When we are young, our bodies can absorb some of these hostilities, but as we get older we lose that ability. Consequently the body breaks down in some of the vital areas, causing ulcers, high blood pressure, colitis, arthritis, heart trouble, headaches, kidney stones, gallstones, and a host of other illnesses.

One day I visited County Hospital in San Diego to call on a 72-year-old minister hospitalized due to a severe case of glaucoma. He was basically a fine man who loved God and wanted to serve Him, but like many Christians, he had never really dealt with his sin of anger. When I arrived in his room, I was ill prepared for the angry tirade that erupted in my direction. He proceeded unceremoniously to downgrade the medical profession in general and the doctors and nurses of County Hospital in particular. After a few moments he literally became livid with rage. Clasping him by the wrist, I shook him and exclaimed, "Paul if you don't stop this, you're going to kill yourself!" Little did I realize that within two days he would drop dead of a heart attack, though he had never experienced one before and had not been confined to the hospital for that reason.

Several months after the funeral I used his case in a sermon illustration. After the service an ophthalmologist in our church said to me, "Just this week I read in a medical journal that protracted hostility is one of the leading causes of glaucoma."

As tragic as the emotional and physical results of anger may be, they can scarcely be compared with the terrible spiritual damage they create. Ephesians 4:30-32 explains it clearly, "And grieve not the holy Spirit of God, whereby ye are sealed unto the day of redemption. Let all bitterness, and wrath, and anger, and clamour, and evil speaking, be put away from you, with all malice: And be ye kind one to another, tenderhearted, forgiving one another, even as God for Christ's sake hath forgiven you." If I were to ask, How does a person grieve the Holy Spirit of God? you would probably reply with a list of overt sins such as adultery or murder, but these verses make it clear that grieving the Holy Spirit takes place in the mind through anger.

It is impossible for a Christian to enjoy his spiritual resources if he grieves the Holy Spirit. In the previous chapter we saw that the Spirit of Christ or the Holy Spirit comes into a person's life when invited. This gives an individual the capacity to overcome his weaknesses and cure such a malady as depression. *But victory is not automatic!* In order for a Christian to secure the victory, he must cooperate with the Holy Spirit. That means that he must not indulge in the mental sin of anger.

Anger is the sin that besets more Christians and probably causes more spiritual defeat than any other sin, and severely limits God's use of an individual's life.

It grieves the Spirit of God and keeps him a spiritual pigmy throughout his life. It not only minimizes his usefulness to God, but it compounds his emotional maladies.

## God's Cure for Anger

Secular man proposes no meaningful cure for anger. A young man came in for counseling one day acknowledging that he had visited a psychiatrist on six occasions. The diagnosis given to him was, "I hate my mother." This hatred of his mother tied his stomach in knots, raised the hair on the back of his arm on occasion, and created the initial wave of marital disharmony in his home. "If you have been to see a psychiatrist and he told you that your tensions were produced by hatred of your mother, why did you come to me?" I asked. The young man sadly replied, "He told me what my problem was, but he didn't tell me what to do about it." We should not be surprised that the young man was not instructed how to overcome his anger, for without God's power in one's life, there is no cure. One psychiatrist in a *Reader's Digest* article offered this typically secular suggestion. An angry-prone person, he advised, would be wise to analytically chart what sets off his anger and accordingly avoid it. Escapism usually become the recourse of secular man who refuses to avail himself of the power of God. In response to the above psychiatrist's suggestion, we may well counter, "What if anger is occasioned by your wife, your children, your job, your neighbors, or planet earth?" It is impossible for man to avoid everything that irritates him. Therefore, God offers a better remedy. Consider the following five steps, which I have shared with hundreds of people, many of whom have experienced their first relief by using this formula.

(1) *Admit that your anger is sin.* As long as you excuse anger, you are incurable! After twenty-five years in the counseling room I think I have heard just about all of them. One man complained, "I am a German choleric." Another Christian worker, whose anger had

caused him to be dropped from a mission board, told me, "I come from a Syrian background; my father and mother are angry, my entire family is angry." Another man explained, "My father and mother had ulcers from being angry, my sister and brother had ulcers—how could I be anything but angry?" Although all of these people were seriously in error, I can appreciate their feeling because for the first thirty-six years of my life, I lamented, "I'm Scotch, French, and Irish; who wouldn't be angry?"

All of this is subterfuge in a misguided attempt to cover up the fact that we have sinned. Until man calls anger sin and stops trying to justify it, his plight is hopeless. Through the years it has been my privilege to help many angry people, but in the process I have failed to assist numerous others. I find one common thread winding through the files of the latter: they refused to admit they were angry people, but insisted on justifying their sin.

Only by facing your anger as a sin will you ever cure it. That is the first giant step toward victory.

Repeatedly people in the counseling room tell me, "If my husband would change, I wouldn't be angry," or "It's my wife that sets me off." They have not yet learned that victory in Christ is not contingent upon other people's behavior, but on Christ alone.

(2) *Confess your sin of anger to God.* Like any other sin, anger can be forgiven and cured. First John 1:9 promises that "If we confess our sins, he is faithful and just to forgive us our sins, and to cleanse us from all unrighteousness." The sooner you recognize your anger and confess it, the sooner you will obtain victory over it.

(3) *Ask God to take away the habit pattern of anger.* First John 5:14, 15 assures us that if we ask anything according to the will of God, He not only hears us but also answers our requests. Since we know it is not God's will that we be angry, we can be assured of victory if we ask Him to take away the habit pattern. Although secular man may be a slave to habit, the Christian is not. We are admittedly victims of habit,

but we need not remain slaves to habit when we have at our disposal the power of the Spirit of God.

(4) *Give thanks for God's mercy, grace, and power*. We need to follow up our request for victory over the habit pattern of anger by thanking God for His mercy and forgiveness in the face of our failure. We must then thank Him that we have within us His Holy Spirit for by His power we can experience a reversal of this habit pattern.

(5) *Repeat this formula every time you are angry*. It would be idealistic to assume that invoking this formula only once would change a lifetime habit of anger. It is much more practical to face the fact anger will occur even after your first use of the formula. The ultimate victory, however, comes with repetition. Quickly follow your sin with a prayer of confession, asking God to change the habit pattern and give thanks by faith for what He is going to do in your life. As one man admitted after trying this formula for a few weeks, "I had to confess my anger the first day at least 1,000 times, but the next day was better; I only had to do it 997 times. Now, however, anger is gradually becoming a thing of the past." In my opinion this man provides a practical case study for those who gain victory over anger. I have met no one who experienced an instant cure. Instead, it comes by conscious and repetitive attention, combined with the gradual exercise of new mental habit patterns.

After speaking on this subject several years ago, I was asked by an elderly gentleman, "Do you think it is possible for a man who has been angry for seventy years to break the habit?" In response, strictly by faith, I replied, "God's power is available to you and can cure any habit." Two years later, while speaking in a nearby city, I spotted him and his wife in the audience. After the meeting he said, "I want to give you a progress report. God has cured my problem of anger. If you don't believe it, ask my wife." I could see by the expression on her face that she was ready to testify that he had experienced the life-changing power of God. Literally hundreds of other testimonials like this could validate that the power of the Holy Spirit of God is able to put love in the heart of any angry-prone person who is willing to let Him. *When love replaces anger, depression cannot possibly intrude.*

# 8

# Self-Pity and Depression

At last we have come to the primary cause of depression. In spite of the causes listed previously, nothing produces depression faster or more deeply than self-pity.

Whenever I confront a depressed person with this cause for depression, he invariably resists me, usually protesting, "I never feel sorry for myself!" or "That may be true most of the time, but my case is different." One lady angrily retorted, "I came to you for help, but I can see you don't understand my problem!" Some people even stalk out in a huff and slam the door.

The truth, like surgery, hurts. There is simply no way to have a tumor removed without pain. The same is true emotionally. The moment we call the tumor of self-pity to the attention of a depressed person, he resists it. But that doesn't change anything! In fact, I never expect agreement on this point from one who is depressed. In his condition, anything as ugly as self-pity is simply too much to bear. He would much rather receive sympathy, pills, or pious platitudes that place the responsibility on someone else.

I have repeatedly noted that non-depressed people seem to accept this diagnosis easily. Even individuals usually prone to depression, when not depressed, seldom argue. It is the depressed themselves who seem to rebel against it. Fortunately, most people upon reflection will acknowledge the problem and take steps to cure it. Of one thing I am certain: if the mental thinking pattern of self-pity is not arrested, the person is hopeless; the more he indulges in self-pitying thoughts, the deeper the depression becomes.

Even medication or electric-shock therapy can only offer temporary periods of relief. If the mental thought patterns are not changed, the person soon returns to his depression.

Various excuses are offered by the depressed who refuse to face self-pity as a possible cause for their miseries. The intellectual or highly educated often protest, "That's too simple! It must be more complex." Others refuse to approach a counselor who provides his counselees with such an analysis. One woman has suffered with depression for more than seven years, but she has steadfastly refused to see me. Her reason is quite simple. She has read the chapter on depression in my book *Spirit-Controlled Temperament,* where I briefly dealt with the problem. She tells her friends, "I know he would say that I'm feeling sorry for myself, and I know that isn't true. My problem is much deeper than that." I am convinced she could have known deliverance years ago if she had just faced the problem honestly.

## Rare—If Any Exceptions

I have not written this book sooner because I wanted more time to study the problem. Except for *Spirit-Controlled Temperament* I have not seen anything in print that places the primary blame for depression on self-pity. Since the book was published eight years ago, hundreds of counselors, pastors, and formerly depressed individuals have indicated their agreement. In addition, I have expanded this theme before thousands of people in family seminars. Although some have taken issue with me at first, many letters in my files strongly confirm the principle.

A few weeks ago I returned to a city in which I had directed a seminar the previous year. A woman conceded, "Last year I was so angry at your suggestion that self-pity was responsible for my depression that I stalked out of the seminar before it was over, but a friend bought your cassette tape on the subject and insisted I hear it. As I began tracing my thought patterns prior to the depression, I realized that I really was feeling sorry for myself. Honest confrontation of that fact has changed my life."

I do not enjoy telling depressed people that they are indulging in self-pity. In fact, on one occasion I felt downright unpatriotic. While holding a family conference in a midwestern city, I was requested by a pastor to counsel one of the women in his congregation. As she walked into the room, I remember thinking, "She is the thinnest woman I have ever seen." She had lost thirty-nine pounds during the previous six months and weighed only eighty-nine pounds. Her husband was an Air Force officer shot down over North Vietnam, officially reported as "missing in action."

As she sobbed out her story, I almost wept with her. For four years she had not known what to prepare for mentally. Was her husband alive or dead? Each day her three small sons would ask, "Mommy, do you think our daddy is alive?" Finally she broke down and sobbed, "I'd rather know he was dead than face this constant uncertainty!" If ever I was tempted to offer a person sympathy in the counseling room, it was this woman. As a basic rule I never sympathize with depressed people. Compassion, understanding, and help are appropriate, but these people have already pitied themselves excessively, thus generating their depression. What they need is help, which comes by gently getting them to see that they are indulging in self-pity.

When I asked this dear lady if she loved her husband, she replied, "Yes! He and my boys are the only things in life that are important to me." I then drew her attention to the fact that her previous statement indicated greater love for herself than for her husband. "Is mental certainty really more important to you than the possibility your husband is alive?" She sat up straight and exclaimed, "O God, I've let myself get so upset that I'm not thinking straight anymore!" That woman changed her entire life style by altering her mental attitude. Her circumstances did not change, for her husband remained an M.I.A. Instead of feeling sorry for herself, however, she began to give thanks that she did not know her husband was dead. Her genuine love for him soon took precedence over her love for herself, and she communicated that thought to her sons. As they asked questions about their father, she led them in prayer that wherever he was, he would be strong and look forward to seeing them all again.

The prospect of this goal lifted that entire family out of the slough of despondence and depression. Only by claiming God's grace and giving thanks in the face of the circumstances could they face their uncertain future.

It is not difficult to analyze this case as a classic example of the dangers of self-pity. All Americans can sympathize with this woman. We can also feel her anger and bitterness because of the injustice of the Viet Cong, whose treatment of P.O.W.s will stand in the annals of history among the most inhumane treatment extended to mankind in modern times. One may get all worked up by the sheer barbarity of these people, but such anger and hostility will simply lead to self-pity, and that self-pity will produce depression.

## The Depression Formula

Seldom in life do we reduce an emotional problem to a formula, but in the case of depression it is possible. Consider the following:

INSULT
or
INJURY + ANGER × SELF-PITY = DEPRESSION
or
REJECTION

The validity of that formula has been confirmed hundreds of times, both in and out of the counseling room. On a flight from Mobile to Atlanta I was pressed between two businessmen. Absorbed in writing this book, I nevertheless could sense the fifty-year-old oil company executive seated by the window reading my manuscript. Finally he apologized and said, "I wonder if you could explain something about depression to me. For the first twenty-two years of our marriage my wife had almost never been depressed, but eight years ago, after the birth of our last child, she became seriously depressed. We have spent a fortune on doctors, psychiatrists and electro-shock treatments, but she is getting worse. Now I find that I am becoming depressed because she is."

The obvious question was the right one as I asked, "Did your wife want to get pregnant eight years ago?" "No," he replied, "she was very resentful all during the pregnancy and has never forgiven me for it." I would be very surprised if her depression had been caused by some mysterious birth problem or menopausal chemical imbalance. Consider the formula applied to that woman:

UNWANTED PREGNANCY + RESENTMENT ×
SELF-PITY = DEPRESSION

The fact that her depression didn't go away but got worse is evidence of the fact that it was self-pity, not a malfunction of the glands. The more she felt sorry for herself, the worse her depression became. Consider his identical formula:

DEPRESSED WIFE + RESENTMENT ×
SELF-PITY = DEPRESSION

One day as my wife and I were returning to San Diego from a seminar, a very personable stewardess kept watching as I was working on this manuscript. Finally her curiosity got the best of her and she asked, "What are you writing so furiously?" When I told her it was a book on *How to Win Over Depression,* she spontaneously replied, "Hurry and finish it—I need to read it right now!" My response to this girl who looked like she didn't have a care in the world was, "How could you at twenty-two have anything to be depressed about?" Instantly her resentments spilled out. "This airline is inconsiderate! We are short-handed on this flight and they forgot to stock it properly, so we can't give halfway decent service." When I explained to her that resentment $\times$ self-pity $=$ depression, she said, "Oh, I'll be all right when I get on the beach where I can hear the waves lapping up on the shore. It seems to soothe my jangled nerves." At the risk of being considered obnoxious, I felt I should warn her that if she didn't stop indulging in self-pity, one of these days she would no longer be able to hear the roar of the waves over her mental bitterness. "But I can't quit," she blurted out. That is when I introduced her to Jesus Christ, who is able to straighten out our faulty thinking patterns.

Depression-inducing self-pity seems to be no respecter of persons. It ambushes intellectuals and nonintellectuals with equal treachery. One brilliant but depressed scholar I know holds a Ph.D. degree and has developed a world-renowned reputation. He had as a young man offered great promise and was expected by those in his field to excel. Having a problem marriage, he drifted into serious patterns of hostility toward his wife. These, in turn, caused him to indulge in the habit pattern of self-pity, which demotivated him. After years of such thinking, he came in for counseling. Having written few articles and never finishing a book, this brilliant man had wasted the creativity potential of a lifetime. Naturally he blamed his wife instead of himself. "If it hadn't been for that woman, I could have realized my potential." Instead of reproaching her for his lack of motivation, he ultimately had to face the fact that *he* was responsible. Actually, he spent so much time feeling sorry for himself that he had no mental space or emotional inspiration to be creative.

Another illustration of the depression formula entered my office and sighed, "After eight months of marriage, I'm as frigid as an iceberg." This lovely young woman had married a handsome marine in our city some eight months before. They had been madly in love, according to her report, and she had looked forward to their wedding with great joy. Depressed after only a few months of marriage, she lost all interest in her husband. It seems that this young woman had been accused of promiscuity by a stepmother when she was fourteen years old. Two of her older sisters were very loose in their morals prior to marriage, which had caused the family no end of shame. When the stepmother made her untrue accusation, the girl mentally promised herself, "I will be a virgin when I marry, no matter what." Unfortunately, when her handsome fiancé put the engagement ring on her finger and they set their wedding date, she let down her barriers and they had intercourse. She admitted to enjoying it and practicing it several times before the wedding.

Her problems really began when she donned her beautiful white wedding gown for the first time. That was her first genuine reminder that she was entering marriage without her virginity. The more she thought about it, the angrier she became. Instead of blaming herself for giving in, she placed all the blame on her husband. Self-justification is a natural defense mechanism against self-condemnation, of course, so it was easier to blame him than share the responsibility. Before long her hostility produced self-pity, and finally she became depressed. Her doctor prescribed medication that merely afforded temporary relief. The only hope for that young woman was to forgive her husband, forgive herself, and seek God's forgiveness for her sins. When she finally did that, she was not only able to rid herself of depression, but to experience a renewed love for her husband. Since that time they have effected a warm and meaningful relationship together.

## You Don't Need a Change of Circumstances

Most people insist that a change in circumstances would begin an end to their depression. Unfortunately, that provides only temporary relief. If a change of circumstances does not convert one's thinking pattern, depression will recur. One woman, married four times, admitted that the best husband was really her first. After being depressed with four different men, she was finally willing to admit that *she* was the problem, not the husbands.

## Self-Pity Is a Sin

When stripped of its false facade of excuse-making and self-justification, self-pity stands naked and exposed as a mental attitude sin. Those who would be most hesitant to commit an overt act of sin such as adultery or fornication seem to have no compunction against this mental sin.

Self-pity is really a denial of the biblical principle that "all things work together for good to them that love God, to them who are the called according to his purpose" (Rom. 8:28). That verse does not state that all things are good, but that all things *work together* for good. There is a vast difference. God can use everything in our life for good, if for no other reason than to get us to look to Him for guidance when we are faced with the frustrating problems of life. For that reason it is imperative that once a person has faced self-pity as sin, he must look to God for grace to face his circumstances. The sooner he builds up his faith by reading and studying the Word of God, and by the filling of the Holy Spirit, the sooner he will experience lasting deliverance.

Once you have received Jesus Christ, you become a child of God (John 1:12). As a member of the family of God, you have a heavenly Father who is not only abundantly able to care for your needs but is infinitely interested in every detail of your life. According to Jesus, He is the God who has numbered the hairs of our head and who sees the sparrow when it falls. Since He is the God who designs the beautiful lilies of the field, Jesus concludes, "Wherefore, if God so clothe the grass of the field, which to day is, and to morrow is cast into the oven, shall he not much more clothe you,

O ye of little faith?" (Matt. 6:30). A Christian should keep in focus the fact that God is interested in every facet of his life and is more than willing to give him victory over his problems.

## Trials Are Not Overwhelming

Every human being faces trials. For some strange reason Christians develop the notion that as Christians they will escape from tribulation. That is just not true. Dr. Henry Brandt, a Christian psychologist, wrote an excellent book entitled *Christians Have Troubles Too*. In it he points out that God has not promised to save us from our problems but to supply our need as we go through our problems. The Apostle Paul had also learned this, for he stated, "My God shall supply all your need according to his riches in glory by Christ Jesus" (Phil. 4:19). D. L. Moody labeled that verse "God's blank check," because it provides a supernatural provision for every human need.

Trials are never overwhelming; they just seem that way. First Corinthians 10:13 explains, "There hath no temptation (trial) taken you but such as is common to man: but *God is faithful,* who will not suffer you to be tempted above that ye are able; but will with the temptation (trial) also make a way to escape, that ye may be able to bear it." Any Christian at a given point in time can undergo a common trial of life, but with the absolute confidence that it will not be so overwhelming that he breaks under it. God knows your limitations. As evangelist Ken Poure says, "That is the guarantee that our trials are 'Father Filtered.' " In other words, every trial that comes into your life is filtered by the heavenly Father. He sees to it that the problem is not so large that it will crush you. Most Christians, however, are not content to accept the grace of God when they enter the furnace of trial. Instead, they demand immediate deliverance or request a path which bypasses all affliction.

Nobody takes pleasure in the testing of life, but

James 1:2, 3 prescribes, "Count it all joy when ye fall into divers temptations" for "the trying of your faith worketh patience." This is the way we grow up spiritually and emotionally.

People are like steel: they are soft unless tested. Your tests in life are an essential part of your tempering process. As we have seen, you are never tested above your ability to endure. Oh, you may be tried beyond your desires, but God knows your mettle, He diagrams your future, and He knows exactly what you need. Therefore, the Word of God instructs us that instead of griping and groaning and feeling sorry for ourselves, which only produces depression, we are advised to "count it all joy."

One depressed woman spent most of her time in the counseling room dissecting her husband. Nothing he did seemed to please her. In an excessive expression of self-pity she exclaimed, "Why couldn't I have married a kind and gentle man like Mrs. K. . . .'s down the street. Her husband is considerate, thoughtful and respectful to her as a woman." Knowing the counselee's husband as I did, fully aware that he was surly, inconsiderate, and unkind to everyone, I still had to offer an encouraging reply. In all honesty I could assert, "God's grace is sufficient for you." I then proceeded to explain that the greater her problem, the greater the grace. "The lady down the street does not have a sizable problem to live with and she does not merit much grace from God. But since you face such an enormous problem, you will be granted more grace to cope with it." Instantly the woman snapped, "I'd rather have the kind husband than the grace!"

Her response is not unusual, though refreshingly honest. Most people would rather avoid the trials of life than obtain the grace to face them.

It should be of great comfort to us that all problems are filtered by the Father. That is, before they ever come our way, He has measured whether or not we are able to endure them, guaranteeing that He will "with the (testing) also make a way to escape!" When confronting a testing, you must make a distinctive choice. You can either respond with anger and bitterness over the problem and then indulge in self-pity, which will induce depression, or you can look to God, your heavenly Father, thank Him by faith for His power and grace to pass through the trial, and then lean upon His everlasting arms. You must make the decision. But of this you can be certain: yielding to self-pity will assuredly lead to depression.

## Crises—Trials and Stress

The way you face the crises and trials of life often determines your state of health. Dr. Thomas Holmes, professor of psychiatry at the University of Washington School of Medicine in Seattle, has actually worked out a system that shows how much stress each crisis in life creates. In an article in the *Chicago Tribune*, July 18, 1972,[1] he explained that after twenty-five years of study he has compiled a list of 43 of the most common stress-producing experiences of life. He has attributed a point score from 100 down to 11 according to the severity of the stress on an individual's emotions caused by the crisis. As you read his list, consider the fact that no human being can escape all of these crises (and hopefully, no human being is going to experience all of them!).

| Rank | Crisis | Points |
|------|--------|--------|
| 1. | Death of a spouse | 100 |
| 2. | Divorce | 73 |
| 3. | Marital separation | 65 |
| 4. | Jail term | 63 |
| 5. | Death of close family member | 63 |
| 6. | Personal injury or illness | 53 |
| 7. | Marriage | 50 |
| 8. | Job firing | 47 |
| 9. | Marital reconciliation | 45 |
| 10. | Retirement | 45 |

[1] "Your Emotional Stresses Can Make You Sick," *Chicago Tribune*, July 18, 1972, section 1, pp. 1ff. Reprinted, courtesy of the *Chicago Tribune*.

| Rank | Crisis | Points |
|------|--------|--------|
| 11. | Change in health of family member | 44 |
| 12. | Pregnancy | 44 |
| 13. | Sexual difficulties | 39 |
| 14. | Gain of new family member | 39 |
| 15. | Business readjustment | 39 |
| 16. | Change in financial state | 38 |
| 17. | Death of close friend | 37 |
| 18. | Change to different line of work | 36 |
| 19. | Change in number of arguments with spouse | 35 |
| 20. | Mortgage more than $10,000 | 31 |
| 21. | Foreclosure of mortgage or loan | 30 |
| 22. | Change in responsibilities at work | 29 |
| 23. | Departure of son or daughter from home | 29 |
| 24. | Trouble with in-laws | 29 |
| 25. | Outstanding personal achievement | 28 |
| 26. | Wife's beginning or stopping work | 26 |
| 27. | Beginning or end of school | 26 |
| 28. | Change in living conditions | 25 |
| 29. | Change of personal habits | 24 |
| 30. | Trouble with boss | 23 |
| 31. | Change in work hours or conditions | 20 |
| 32. | Change in residence | 20 |
| 33. | Change in schools | 20 |
| 34. | Change in recreation | 19 |
| 35. | Change in church activities | 19 |
| 36. | Change in social activities | 18 |
| 37. | Mortgage or loan less than $10,000 | 17 |
| 38. | Change in sleeping habits | 16 |
| 39. | Change in number of family gatherings | 15 |
| 40. | Change in eating habits | 15 |
| 41. | Vacation | 13 |
| 42. | Christmas | 12 |
| 43. | Minor violations of the law | 11 |

Dr. Holmes then established an illness predictor scale showing that there was a high risk potential of developing major illnesses within a two-year period after accumulating a certain number of stress points accordingly.

## ILLNESS PREDICTOR SCALE

|  | Total Points |
|---|---|
| **LOW** | 150 |
|  | 175 |
|  | 200 |
|  |  |
|  | 225 |
| **MEDIUM** | 250 |
|  | 275 |
|  | 300 |
|  |  |
| **HIGH** | 325 |
|  | 350 |
|  | 375 |

According to the above chart, there is a high degree of possibility that you will be physically ill if you collect as many as 300 or more points within a resasonably short time. For example, if a person loses his partner and out of loneliness rushes into a second marriage, he has accumulated 150 points. If he and his wife purchase a home with a mortgage over $10,000 (31 points), if he develops sexual difficulties in the new marriage (39 points) and experiences a job change (36 points) along with the natural change in social activities that a new spouse would cause (18 points), receives a minor traffic violation (11 points), and a disagreement or two with his new wife (35 points), all it would take is Christmas (12 points) or a vacation (13 points) to push him over the precipice of accumulated stress points that could induce illness.

Is it realistic to blame this illness on these crises

or changes in one's life style? Closer examination indicates that the real culprit is one's mental attitude toward these circumstances of life, not the trials or crises themselves. You have doubtless seen individuals go through similar experiences seemingly unscathed emotionally, whereas you have also seen others thrown into a despondent or despairing state of depression by only one of them. Consequently, we are confronted again with the fact that more important than the crises of life is the mental attitude with which we face them.

An interesting observation about Dr. Holmes' stress-producing experiences was made by my secretary. After laboriously putting all forty-three of these events and their ratings on a visual transparency to be used with my lectures, she said, "The one thing these experiences all have in common is change." If you read over the list, you will agree. Subconsciously most of us dislike change, but who can possibly avoid it? In fact, life would be rather dull and boring if we didn't experience change once in a while. It is not the change that produces the problem; the person with a good mental attitude can thrive on such change, but the person who gripes verbally or in his mind about the change and feels sorry for himself that it became necessary will have trouble. Some people have such a poor mental attitude that they can get depressed just by the thought of impending change.

The error of the depressed-prone person is that his thought patterns are too inward. Everything in life is scrutinized from a self-centered point of view. For that reason the slightest insult, affront, or difficulty can send him into a state of depression. Only by recognizing self-pity as a sin and dealing with it forthrightly is he ever going to have lasting victory over this insidious habit that will destroy him spiritually, mentally, emotionally, and physically.

The importance of mental attitude can be seen by studying the following chart showing the characteristics of the three kinds of depression. By following the progression from mental, physical, emotional, and spiritual, you can trace the effects of improper thoughts on your entire nature.

## CHARACTERISTICS OF THE THREE KINDS OF DEPRESSION.

|  | *Discouragement* (mild) | *Despondency.* (serious) | *Despair* (severe) |
|---|---|---|---|
| Mental: | Self-doubt<br>Resentment<br>Self-pity | Self-criticism<br>Anger<br>Self-pity | Self-rejection<br>Bitterness<br>Self-pity |
| Physical: | Loss of appetite<br>Sleeplessness<br>Unkempt<br>  appearance | Apathy<br>Hypochondria<br>"Weeps" | Withdrawal<br>Passivity<br>Catatonia |
| Emotional: | Discontent<br>Sadness<br>Irritability | Distress<br>Sorrow.<br>Loneliness | Hopelessness<br>Schizophrenia<br>Abandonment |
| Spiritual: | Question's<br>  God's will<br>Displeased with<br>  God's will<br>Ungrateful<br>Unbelieving | Anger at<br>  God's will<br>Rejects<br>  God's will<br>Gripes about<br>  God's will | Resentment<br>  to Word<br>Indifferent<br>  toward Word<br>Unbelief in<br>  the Word |

THE DEPRESSION — FREE MAN

# 9

# How to Overcome Self-Pity

Self-pity is not only a sin, but also a habit. The more it is indulged in, the easier it is for an individual to shift into this thinking pattern whenever disagreeable circumstances confront him. Most of the things we do in life are the result of habit. Certain instincts combined with environmental circumstances produce habit. The more we follow an established pattern, the more ingrained it becomes in our behavior. Habit is simply a form of what psychologists label "conditioned response."

We must constantly remind ourselves that we are not slaves to habit, even though most people think they are. Studies have proved that habits can be broken. One researcher concludes that any practice you indulge in for thirty-nine days becomes a habit; similarly, any activity you discontinue for thirty-nine days becomes a broken habit. While this may be true for such things as jogging, smoking, or drinking coffee, I seriously question the validity of that suggestion regarding self-pity, because you may go thirty-nine days without an occasion for self-pity. But it does highlight the fact that a modification of a thinking pattern over a protracted period of time can thwart one's self-pitying thought habits which produce depression.

I have shared the following formula for overcoming self-pity with many depressed-prone individuals. Those who have been willing to follow it have found great relief. Those who preferred to indulge in the "pleasure" of self-pity have not been helped. (As startling as it may seem, self-pity is a pleasurable mental exercise to many people, although the consequences of depression are not so pleasant.)

(1) *Face self-pity as a sin.* "Do all things without murmurings and disputings" (Phil. 2:14). Facing self-pity as a sin is the initial step toward victory over this cruel slave-driver. This is probably the hardest step, for, humanly speaking, self-pity is so easy to justify. In the courtroom of your mind during times of distress you are the judge, jury, and prosecuting attorney. Perry Mason never had a more cooperative listening audience. But instead of commiserating with yourself and blaming other people for the insult, injury, rejection, or tragedy, face self-pity squarely as a giant mental sin that will destroy you.

Unless you severely judge self-pity as sin, you will never break the habit. The person who justifies self-pity is like the alcoholic who refuses to face his condition as an alcoholic. You cannot break any strong habit until you are willing to admit its evil control over you.

Never excuse self-pity! Humanly speaking, you will find this easy to do. You may have been rejected by your parents or betrayed by a Judas whom you trusted, you may have a deplorable job with no apparent chance for advancement, or you may find yourself married to a very selfish, insensitive, and inconsiderate partner. You may even suffer from a serious physical impairment or be isolated from everyone you love. Surely human wisdom admits these and other such problems in life as just cause for self-pity. But be sure of this: self-pity will create depression whether the cause is justified or imagined.

In addition, the sin of unbelief from which self-pity springs will keep you from drawing on the power of God's Holy Spirit at your time of need. Even though you are a child of God, when you quench or grieve the Holy Spirit by self-pity, you become as powerless as those who are not Christians. For that reason the sooner you label the thinking pattern of self-pity as sin, the sooner you will take your first step toward recovery.

(2) *Confess self-pity as a sin.* "If we confess our sins, he is faithful and just to forgive us our sins, and to cleanse us from all unrighteousness" (1 John 1:9). Our heavenly Father is a merciful God, ready to forgive whenever sinners confess their sins in the name of His Son Jesus Christ. The word "confess" literally means to agree with God that it is sin and should have no place in our thinking pattern. The sooner you confess the sin of self-pity, the sooner you take your second step toward curing this self-destroying habit.

(3) *Ask God for victory over self-pity.* "And this is the confidence that we have in him, that, if we ask any thing according to his will, he heareth us: and if we know that he hear us, whatsoever we ask, we know that we have the petitions that we desired of him" (1 John 5:14, 15). Since God has already pronounced His anathema upon self-pity, we can be sure that if we desire victory, He will provide it. Remember also that the Christian commands resources for overcoming habits not shared by the non-Christian. For that reason I do not hesitate to point out that a Christian does not have to be a slave to this tyrannical habit.

Eleven years ago Dr. Henry Brandt stated to a group of ministers in San Diego, "You can use your background as an excuse for present behavior only until you become a Christian. After that it is no longer a valid excuse for present behavior." When a person receives Jesus Christ, he inherits a new dimension of power created within to provide victory over old habit patterns (2 Cor. 5:17). With all due respect to self-discipline and mental self-control, most people lack the strength of character within themselves to inhibit self-pitying thoughts. However, since the Spirit of Jesus Christ entering "the natural man" provides him with supernatural power through the Holy Spirit, he is abundantly able to achieve victory. The Apostle Paul announced for all of us, "I can do all things through Christ which strengtheneth me" (Phil. 4:13).

(4) *Thank God in the experience that produced self-pity.* "In every thing give thanks: for this is the will of God in Christ Jesus concerning you" (1 Thess. 5:18). Victory is dependent upon this next step! Unless by God's help and in obedience to His command you give thanks in the experience, your self-pity will return and reactivate your depression. It is important to realize that thanksgiving "in every thing" is critical not only because it is required by God to be a Spirit-filled Christian but also, as we shall see in a later chapter, it is emotionally therapeutic.

It is not always possible to thank God *for* the experience, but it is essential to thank God *in* the experience.

## Even Prayer Doesn't Help

You may find it strange that a high percentage of depressed people frequently pray. Their undesirable habit of self-pity and continual griping have alienated them even from their dearest friends. Their verbalized self-pity wears out the most persistent friendship until it seems that only God will pay any attention to them. The severely depressed or despondent person, of course, is apt to feel that even God has turned him off.

You may also be surprised to learn that all prayer is not good. In fact, much of what people call prayer is downright harmful, because it is contrary to the will of God. Most depressed people use their prayer life to nurse their grudges and announce their self-pity. This is not only debilitating but spiritually harmful.

Moses, one of the great Old Testament saints, offered probably the poorest example of a prayer to be found in the Bible. Admittedly very displeased with the children of Israel for their griping, he turned his displeasure upon God and prayed, "Wherefore hast thou afflicted thy servant? and wherefore *have I* not found favour in thy sight, that thou layest the burden of all this people upon me? *Have I conceived* all this people? *have I begotten them,* that thou shouldest say unto me, Carry them in thy bosom, as a nursing father beareth the sucking child, unto the land which thou swarest unto their fathers? Whence should I have flesh to give unto all this people? for they weep unto me, saying, Give us flesh, that we may eat. *I am not able to bear all this people alone,* because it is *too heavy for me.* And if thou deal thus with me, *kill me,* I pray thee, out of hand, if I have found favour in thy sight; *and let me not see my wretchedness"* (Num. 11:11-15, italics mine).

During the course of his prayer, which began in anger and progressed in self-pity, Moses became so depressed that he actually asked God to let him die. Poor Moses! Resenting the clamor of the people and his leadership, he disregarded God's supernatural supply of his needs. Such prayer will always leave a person depressed.

A minister friend shared with me the results of a survey on prayer made while he was in college. A large number of depressed persons with a Christian background were separated into three categories. One group was offered counseling on a group and individual basis in methods of improving their mental attitude. The second group met together for prayer with an instructor who showed them how to pray properly. The third group was told to go home and pray. After several weeks almost fifty percent of those who were counseled had improved. Of those who prayed together on a weekly basis under the guidance of a biblically oriented instructor, eighty-five percent were helped. But of those who prayed privately without instruction, not one improved, and several showed deterioration. Upon investigation it was found that every uninstructed person had indulged in the sin of self-pity in his prayer life. No wonder their depression increased.

## Pray With Thanksgiving

To be profitable, prayer must include thanksgiving. The Bible admonishes, "Be careful (anxious) for nothing; but in every thing by prayer and supplication with thanksgiving let your requests be made known unto God. And the peace of God, which passeth all understanding, shall keep your hearts and minds through Christ Jesus" (Phil. 4:6, 7).

The right kind of prayer is beneficial, but such prayer always includes thanksgiving. If you really believe that God answers prayer and is able to work on your behalf, give thanks before there is any indication of what He will do. That kind of prayer is therapeutic. Prayer without thanksgiving will be detrimental and tend to make you depressed. Any time you come away from a period of prayer more depressed than when you started, examine your prayer for that missing ingredient —thanksgiving.

Several years ago, when a new car meant more to me than it does today, I learned a valuable lesson. Upon leaving a banquet, I started to open the door of the car for my wife, only to find that someone had backed into my one-month-old car, caving in one-fourth of the side. For a moment my blood ran cold, my stomach sank, and rather ugly thoughts ran through my mind. But looking up into the sky, I said, "Praise the Lord!" Even though I didn't understand why it happened and it remains a mystery to this day, I wanted to be obedient to God, so I thanked Him by faith, as He commanded in such circumstances. As a result I have never felt bad about the accident. That certainly is not the way I would have felt had I not given thanks.

That situation underscored the principle that one need not understand or even enjoy an experience to give thanks for it. But when faced with an unexpected circumstance in life, you create your own emotional state by either griping or giving thanks.

(5) *Ask to be filled with the Holy Spirit.* "If ye then, being evil, know how to give good gifts unto your children: how much more shall your heavenly Father give the Holy Spirit to them that ask him?" (Luke 11: 13).

Now that you are a clean vessel, having faced and confessed your sin, having asked God for removal of the habit pattern, and by faith thanked Him in the experience, you are in a spiritual position to be filled with the Holy Spirit. "How often should you ask to be filled with the Spirit?" is a question I am frequently asked. My answer is, "Every time you are conscious you are not filled." Ephesians 5:18 makes it clear that we should be continually in the process of being filled with His Spirit.

(6) *Repeat the above formula whenever self-pity recurs.* Educators tell us that repetition is an aid to learning. I have found repetition to be an essential ingredient in gaining victory over habits. It is unrealistic to expect the mental habit of self-pity to vanish immediately, and thus it will take many applications of this formula to insure consistent victory. But the sooner you follow your self-pity with this formula, the sooner you will experience protracted periods of victory.

Do not expect your triumph over self-pity to be a miracle of God's grace without your cooperation. Many depressed people, even after admitting the cause for their depression, want God to take away the thinking pattern without any effort from them. On some occasions I have actually seen people get angry with God because He didn't miraculously subtract their thinking mechanism of self-pity. However, God does not do for us what according to His Word He expects us to do for ourselves. Instead, He exhorts us to cooperate with the Holy Spirit, who enables us to do whatever He commands.

Victory over self-pity and thus over depression can be yours as a Christian, but only if you avail yourself of the spiritual resources that the Spirit-filled life provides. (For a thorough description of how to be filled with the Spirit, see the author's book, *Spirit-Controlled Temperament.*)

### Physician, Heal Thyself

In the introduction to this book I confessed that on October 7, 1969, I experienced the first real depression of my adult life. Since that time there have been three other occasions that provided me a personal opportunity to evaluate this formula for overcoming the self-pity that produces depression.

Our growing church bought forty acres of property in the heart of San Diego to relocate our entire ministry of church, junior and senior high schools, college, and Institute for Creation Research. By faith we paid $500,-000 for this land, which would have provided sixteen usable acres located where two freeways intersect, one of which has a traffic load of 105,000 cars a day—the ideal site in our city for a church.

For three years I had eaten, slept, thought, and dreamed about that development. For months I tramped the streets, lining up adjoining property owners until we owned fifteen lots that would provide access to our land. Somehow local politics and the first wave of eco-logic hysteria combined to oppose the project. For two years we carried on a running battle with city hall. We spent thousands of dollars on lawyers' fees, and an equal amount of legal man hours were donated by in-terested lawyers in the congregation. I had absolutely no doubt our plans would be approved. Naive as I was, the thought that our city fathers would be more in-terested in authorizing 200 tax-paying condominiums to be built there instead of a church had never occurred to me. Consequently, when their vote flashed on the screen showing that our application for a zone variance was defeated, I was stunned.

People began milling around, but I could hardly move—I was numb to the bone! Eventually I mustered enough strength to leave as discreetly as possible. When I finally got away from everyone, I drove alone to the property. I didn't have the courage to visit the spot where my wife and I had knelt and claimed that proper-ty for God. Instead, I went out to a lovely vantage point and sat down in the dirt to think. Can you imagine the nature of my first thoughts? I must confess they weren't very pleasant. "Why, Lord? Why did You let this hap-pen? What did I do wrong? I prayed over this place, I walked over it and claimed it, just as others did for theirs. Why did You let this happen? It worked for

Abraham, for some of my minister friends; why hasn't it worked for me?"

I had lots of questions. And the more I griped, the worse I felt. After two hours I was so miserable I decided it was time to leave. When I climbed the hill we wanted to cut down, I found my wife waiting to console me. Walking over to her car, I tried to thank her for coming and my voice wouldn't work. Try as I would, I couldn't speak. Finally I just walked away and went for a drive.

For two days I went through the worst siege of depression I have ever experienced. Finally it dawned on me that I had quenched the Holy Spirit and was walking in a very carnal state. The thought came to me, "Here you are, the author of a book with a chapter on how to cure depression, a preacher who challenges Christians not to become depressed—and you are depressed. Why don't you practice what you preach?" After confessing my sins of self-pity, doubt, griping, and questioning God, I began thanking Him. I thanked Him for His power and leading, and that though I didn't know what He was going to do, the problem wasn't really mine but His.

A thrilling thing happened that day. The depression lifted, my spirit began to rise, and a deep peace flooded my heart. During succeeding months, though actively engaged in the search for new property and knocking on every door of opportunity, I gained no more idea of God's plan for our church than I had had on October 7. The thrilling part, however, is that I have not felt the slightest twinge of discouragement as long as I have given thanks by faith that God knew what He was doing, even if I didn't.

For the next two years I tried every conceivable method available to get that project approved. Nothing worked! Little old ladies in tennis shoes bent on preserving every known tree in San Diego County showed up at each hearing. Finally we tried selling the land, only to find that developers were afraid that if a church couldn't gain permission to build on four percent of the land, they would find it difficult to get approval for more. The only thing that was consistent was our $55,000 a year annual payments.

During that time I had three other bouts with depression. In each case self-pity set me up for defeat. Oh, I could justify it—hadn't I stepped out by faith? Didn't we need a new church? Our three morning services were filled to capacity, we didn't have enough parking space, and people were being turned away. All that kind of thinking did was make me depressed!

Each time I recognized the depression and applied the formula given above, I got relief. My usual light heart and optimistic spirit returned, and I recaptured the excitement of what I consider the greatest vocation in the world—being a minister of the Gospel!

During the summer of 1970 the Lord lifted me out of my last period of depression over this problem. It was then I turned the situation over to Him completely, deciding to quit trying to work it out myself and let Him take care of it. Shortly after that He laid the work of Family Life Seminars on my heart. This ministry has taken me to more than thirty-eight cities in the country, and thousands of families have been helped through our Friday night and Saturday seminars. Frankly, I've been too busy pastoring, traveling, speaking, and writing this book to indulge in self-pity. Consequently, I haven't been depressed.

Since God is always faithful, it occurs to me that you might like to hear what has happened since I started thanking God by faith instead of griping in unbelief. On February 27, 1973 we bought a beautiful thirty-acre Catholic school and church with twenty-eight buildings, including dormitories, kitchen, recreation field, swimming pool, and an auditorium seating 700 people. Competent builders say we couldn't duplicate it for three to five million dollars. Our cost? $1,325,000 —the same price our other property plus development and parking costs would have been—without a single building.

Now we have two churches, one in San Diego, and one in El Cajon, eighteen miles away, which more than doubles our effectiveness. As I walk through the lovely grounds overlooking our new 110,000 square feet of buildings that are immediately available for us, I can thank God by sight. In fact, on occasion I have even felt giddy about the exciting way it has all happened. Obviously it was a sinful act of unbelief and a waste of my time to be depressed back in 1969 and 1970. God knows what He is doing with our lives. Happy is the Christian who can trust Him by giving thanks even when everything looks black. That is the real key to depression-free living.

# 10

# Depression and Your Mind

The human mind is easily the world's most amazing mechanism. Yet we consistently waste its phenomenal potential, for scientists report that the average person never uses more than ten percent of his brain.

Dr. Gerhard Dirks, possessor of more patents for the IBM Computer than any living man (over fifty of them), told me personally, "I got most of my ideas for the computer by studying the human mind." And someone has observed, "If scientists could build a computer that equaled the feats of the human mind, it would take a structure the size of the Empire State Building to house it."

## Conscious vs. Subconscious

The brain is divided into two main sections—the conscious and the subconscious. We have accumulated considerable knowledge about the conscious, but we know little about the subconscious. In the last few years careful studies have turned up some intriguing concepts, especially one that postulates that we never forget anything we have seen, felt, heard, tasted, or smelled. Of course, the trick is to remember at the right time! But you can be sure that your present likes, dislikes, feelings, and reactions are etched on the record of your subconscious mind, particularly those mental transcriptions made during the impressionable days of your youth.

Another recent discovery about the mind claims that you are influenced more by the subconscious than the conscious. Let me illustrate. Suppose you are fifteen pounds overweight and your conscious mind warns, "Don't eat that piece of fudge; it will make you gain weight." Do you eat it? That depends upon the reaction of your subconscious mind. If it responds, "But I have an unquenchable sweet tooth," "I'm destined to be fat," or "I'm too weak to resist," you will partake.

Now transfer that pattern to the problem of self-pity. Suppose some friend rejects, insults, or injures you. Your conscious mind will caution, "Now don't indulge in self-pity!" (particularly after reading this book) but if your subconscious mind by force of habit retorts, "Everyone treats you like dirt; you're always getting the raw end of the deal" or "You can't trust anyone" or "How could they do that to me after all I've done for them?" you will indulge in self-pity, which follows an unswerving path to depression.

Another important discovery related to the mind concerns the response of the subconscious to the imagination. In fact, the imagination, in my opinion, is the most powerful factor of the mind. Regardless of the vitality of your will power, maintaining a negative image on the screen of your imagination will ultimately break down your will.

A friend of mine is an alcoholic, but for six years he had not touched a drop. One hot day an urgent thought flashed on the screen of his imagination: "An ice cold glass of beer sure would taste good right now." His conscious mind responded, "Don't do it! You're an alcoholic." Because his imagination was visualizing the beer in living three-dimensional color, he talked himself into the assurance that after six years he had learned to control his problem. Within two hours he visited a bar, tried one drink, then another, and you can imagine the rest.

Whenever the will and the imagination come into

conflict, the imagination wins. For this reason self-pity projected on the screen of the imagination is so devastatingly harmful!

On page 66 we saw the influence your mind, will, and heart have on your actions. The will determines what you put in your mind, which in turn activates your feelings and ultimately your conduct, forming a powerful chain reaction:

Will + Mind + Emotions = Actions.

Your will can determine what new material you put into your mind, but it cannot govern your attitude toward the old material, nor can it fully regulate the mind. This is particularly true of the subconscious, which cannot be controlled by the will directly, but may be influenced through the imagination. The governor of your mind is the imagination. As the imagination goes, so goes the mind, both conscious and subconscious.

For illustrative purposes, let us use a movie screen to demonstrate the power of the imagination over both the subconscious and conscious mind.

THE NEGATIVE USE OF IMAGINATION

You can use your imagination either creatively or destructively. Most people, I'm afraid, employ their imagination destructively, for they picture themselves as ineffective, clumsy, fearful, and rejected. If this becomes the governor of their self-image and the inhibitor of their expectations, they may dwell upon the negative experience of the past and look negatively to the future. It is far better to make creative use of the imagination. Only by projecting wholesome and positive images on the screen of your imagination will you rise above the inadequate view of yourself that ensnares most people.

## The Persistence of the Subconscious

Whatever you place on the screen of your subconscious mind will govern your activities! The Bible says, "For as he thinketh in his heart, so is he" (Prov. 23:7). Your imaginative self-image determines how you feel and, as a result, how you work and act. The subconscious mind functions inexorably toward the fulfillment of whatever image you flash on the screen. For that reason you should become a very careful and skillful projectionist.

Exhaustive studies with obese people have brought to light some very interesting uses for creative imagery. Many overweight people who find it difficult to lose weight crave more food the longer they remain on a diet. Whenever they gaze upon sweets, conscious of their effect, they seem powerless to resist. In recent years we have discovered the culprit: the screen of the imagination. When overweight people project an obese image of themselves or an appetizing image of their favorite delicacy, their subconscious mind draws them inexorably toward the fulfillment of that image. Even when their stomach is full, an impelling force entices them to eat. This problem can rarely be changed by the power of the will, but great success has been found in "thinking thin." If they consistently project on the screen of their imagination a picture of themselves as slender and alluring, their subconscious mind will abruptly reject foods that violate that image. Dieting becomes less painful because they gradually lose their craving for foods which conflict with their renewed mental image of themselves.

On several occasions I have suggested this to depressed counselees who were struggling with an obvious weight problem, and many have experienced positive results. I have found that the so-called "happy fat man" is a misnomer; he may be laughing on the outside, but he is grieving on the inside. He simply needs to change his mental image of himself. Only then will he attain lasting success with a diet.

One night in a local ice-cream parlor I saw this graphically illustrated when a woman entered apparently forty-five pounds lighter than when I had counseled her several months before. Rejecting the hot fudge sundae ordered by her friends, she casually requested a plain dish of strawberries. Later she remarked to me, "It's no sacrifice since I have learned to picture myself as thin. Sure, I want the hot fudge sundae, but not nearly as much as I want to be thin." As she spoke, my mind raced back to that day in the counseling room when she confessed to dieting unsuccessfully for almost twenty years. The change in her was not due to will power, but to the discovery of an effective precept: utilize the energy of the imagination to insure desired behavior. Remember, whatever you picture on the screen of your imagination will become the goal toward which your subconscious mind will irresistibly conduct you. The Bible teaches us to cast down "imaginations, and every high thing that exalteth itself against the knowledge of God, and [bring] into captivity *every thought* to the obedience of Christ" (2 Cor. 10:5).

## Creative Imagery and Depression

This principle of controlling your mind, feelings and actions by projecting only beneficial images on the imagination screen of your mind works admirably in the field of depression. People who have tried without success to rid themselves of depression by various therapeutic techniques have tried this method with gratifying results—primarily because it deals with the problem, not the symptoms.

Medication, counseling, electric-shock treatments,

GOD LOVES ME
I can do all things
THRU CHRIST
Self acceptance
THANKSGIVING
Positive Faith

## THE GOOD USE OF IMAGINATION

or other methods will only provide minimal results unless the individual changes the image he projects on the screen of his imagination. Depressed people create a negative, self-pitying picture on the imagination, inevitably making them feel depressed. By creating a fresh, new image they will gradually modify their feeling and their behavior.

A lonely, middle-aged nurseryman came in for counseling after his wife had left him. "She just couldn't stand my long periods of depression any longer," he freely admitted. "I've tried everything, but nothing seems to work." The familiar pattern emerged through his story. Rejected and criticized by a perfectionist father, he felt completely inadequate and apprehensive, incapable of fulfilling his real capabilities. Negative, self-pitying, critical mental images continually projected on the imagination screen of his mind. I challenged him to trust God for a new set of films for his mental projector. As we prayed together I gathered that he had never given God thanks for the qualities and gifts he did possess, and in his prayer he made particular mention of his spirit of ingratitude, but even before he got up off his knees, he thought of three things to be be grateful for, and before he reached the door a slight trace of a smile appeared on his lips. Today, by his own testimony, "I have not been depressed in five years." His wife later explained to a friend why she was able to come back to him. "He isn't the same morose, pessimistic critic I lived with for twenty-three years. He is actually fun to be around."

## Creative Imagery and the Holy Spirit

The Holy Spirit certainly understood the function of the human mind when He inspired man to write the Bible. That is why He never instructed us to think about negative or undesirable things. Instead, the Bible directs us to project only positive thoughts on the screen of our imagination.

Unlike the analyst who leads his patient to "talk out his frustrations" or "recall his childhood experiences," the Bible instructs Christians to forget "those things which are behind" and "to press toward the mark for the prize of the high calling of God in Christ Jesus" (Phil. 3:13, 14).

Instead of thinking about your own inadequacies or failings (real or imagined), "Let this mind be in you, which was also in Christ Jesus" (Phil. 2:5). Rather than indulging in self-pity because some friend has insulted, injured, or rejected you, "Fret not thyself because of evil men" (Prov. 24:19).

The importance of keeping one's mind clear of negative, harmful, and evil thoughts by replacing them with good, wholesome ideas is clearly reflected in Romans 12:2, which challenges Christians to be "transformed by the renewing of your mind." As the mind goes, so goes the behavior! Transformed conduct only follows in the wake of a renewed mind. In other words, exchange your natural (often negative) thinking patterns for the wisdom of God found in the Word of God.

This principle is further illustrated in Romans 8:6, "For to be carnally minded is death; but to be spiritually minded is life and peace." A spiritually minded person will imaginatively project only those things that are pleasing to God. Consequently, he will feel and act in a manner acceptable to God. The Holy Spirit enables us to imagine creatively in those patterns which produce healthy emotions.

## The Power of Suggestion

Never underestimate the influence of suggestion on your mind. It is capable not only of motivating you, but also of activating the glands in your body. Consider, for instance, what happens when you visualize a delicious red apple. Merely picturing that apple on the screen of your imagination arouses your saliva glands until your mouth waters. If you think about it long enough, you can literally "taste that apple."

Did it ever occur to you that depression can be fashioned the same way? Recently an attractive minister's wife drove me to the airport after I had spoken to a group of ministers on the subject of depression. Obviously quite engrossed in the subject, she asked me a question of interest to many women, "Isn't it quite common for women to experience depression when they go through their monthly period?" I responded, "It all depends on whether they expect to be depressed." If a woman anticipates depression each month at this time, she will undoubtedly not be disappointed. This is not to minimize the physiological change within a woman's body, for modern science has awakened us to the fact that a hormonal change can cause an increase in anxiety tendencies and a decrease in energy. But though most women do not like to admit it, those symptoms can be greatly exaggerated and compounded by the power of suggestion.

The minister's wife laughed and added candidly, "I have noticed that when my period comes at a time when I am excited about something else and my mind is occupied with other things, it doesn't have nearly the effect on me that it does at other times." A psychiatrist couldn't have stated it better. If a woman has been trained by her mother to expect debilitation or depression three or four days each month, she will experience it until she reorients her thinking pattern. However, if she has been taught that menstruation is part of God's fantastic design for her life, a symbol of womanhood and motherhood for which she should be grateful, it is less likely to leave her in an apathetic condition.

The same power of suggestion influences the severity of menopause. Many a woman expects to fall apart during her menopause. Rarely is such a woman disappointed! However, women I have met who were determined to face this stage of life as if it were just an ordinary facet of living would not permit themselves to be disabled by it—and they were not.

Your mental attitude is more important in such matters than your hormones and glands because it controls them. Whatever you flash on the imagination screen of your mind will influence your life, starting with the subconscious mind and progressing to the conscious mind and to the function of the glands.

## Six Things That Influence Your Subconscious Mind

(1) *Your imagination*. As we have already illustrated, the imagination may be used negatively or positively to the glory of God. Your task is to direct it.

(2) *Goals*. Most depressed people are obsessed with themselves. It is not enough for the individual to create good mental images of himself, for he must in addition project worthy goals on the screen of his imagination that will lead him to witness the power of God effecting a change in his life. This confronts us with a crucial dilemma: most people think too small. The man of faith always thinks big. And why not? He is a son of the great God whose abundant power is always placed at his disposal. One of Christendom's mighty thinkers, the Apostle Paul, communicated an essential truth in this regard: "My God shall supply all your needs" (Phil. 4:19).

## Despair and Hopelessness

It is no accident that our age of emotional despair and depression is also a time of hopelessness. The younger generation, experiencing an alarming degree of depression, has in many cases given up on their homeland, society, culture, and humanity in general. The Bible warns us that "without a vision, the people perish." Certainly no man can function without vision or a goal. Because the human mind is a goal-oriented mechanism, it must be pursuing an explicit end or it will not function properly. If you do not project on the screen of your imagination a series of worthwhile, challenging goals, you will gradually develop the de-motivating habit of projecting self-defeating, negative, pessimistic goals which will depress you.

## Write Down Your Goals

Probably less than five percent of our population above twenty-one years of age have ever written down their goals. Compare that with a recent statistic indicating that ninety-five percent of the successful businessmen surveyed had drawn up a list of goals to guide them. Putting them down in tangible form helps to etch them more deeply on the screen of our imagination and makes it easier to activate our subconscious mind toward their achievement. Once we have committed our goals to writing, we should make a habit of reading them every day for sixty days.

(3) *Spiritual principles.* The psalmist has said, "Thy word have I hid in mine heart, that I might not sin against thee" (Ps. 119:11). The best way to reverse negative thinking patterns is to memorize scriptural principles that produce happiness. Throughout this book you may have discovered that you are violating certain basic biblical precepts and thus have lost your inner joy. Jesus Christ said, "If you know these things (principles of God), happy are you if you do them." Happiness, then, is the result of:

a. Knowing the principles of God, and
b. Doing them.

As a pastor I have encouraged the members of our congregation on numerous occasions to keep 4" x 6" cards in the flyleaf of their Bible, ready to write down those principles for living particularly suited for their needs. The Word of God is so filled with practical advice that every time you hear it faithfully taught you will discover principles that will meet your heart's special need. The more of them you program into your mind, the easier it is for your subconscious to direct your living habits into those principles that produce a happy life.

(4) *Memory*. We already have mentioned that the human mind never forgets anything. Even though we may not consciously remember something, it can apparently have a spontaneous influence upon us. One woman indicated that she always became depressed when a particular hymn was sung in her church; on some occasions she even had to leave the church service weeping. Later she discovered through a relative that the piece was sung at her mother's funeral. A young girl at the time, she grieved sorely over the loss of her mother and thus, although not recalling the hymn on the conscious level, she subconsciously reacted against it.

Often we are unaware that certain experiences strongly influence our behavior. For this reason we should guard our memory by walking in the Spirit on a consistent basis, for then our memory bank will remain pleasing to God. The individual who indulges in sensual thoughts develops a sensual memory and cultivates sensual appetites. The same is true regarding depression. The individual who dwells upon every distress, every rejection, every loss is naturally liable to depression.

Whenever the memory of such events comes to mind, develop the habit of "forgetting those things which are behind." Refuse to focus upon disagreeable experiences of the past, for they only become more deeply etched on the table of the mind and perpetuate the feelings of sadness or depression. As you consciously look forward to the future with the power and blessing of God, reprogram your mind by looking at difficulties through the eyes of faith, thus replacing negative or self-pitying thought patterns that will subconsciously depress you.

(5) *Habits*. Everyone knows that we are influenced by habits. Since anything you do on a consistent basis becomes easier each successive time, it is essential that you learn constructive thinking habits. The more you think positively about God's blessing in the future, the easier you will maintain an affirmative mental pattern. Naturally, the converse is also true. In Romans 12:2 the Apostle Paul discloses the secret to being "transformed" by "the renewing of your mind." As we renew our mind on the principles of God and create proper habits, the transformed way of life that God promises to every believer becomes readily accessible.

(6) *The Holy Spirit*. One of the special functions of the Holy Spirit is to "bring all things to your remembrance, whatsoever I have said unto you." For this reason it is important for the Christian to read and memorize the Word of God regularly so that the Holy Spirit can bring out of the memory bank those things that God has declared. The Holy Spirit will not bring to your mind anything that God has not said to you, for He relies upon the Word of God to program our minds through hearing, reading, meditating, studying, and memorizing the principles of God. From this storehouse of biblical principles the Holy Spirit can draw out His bountiful riches as we require them. In addition, learning biblical principles for living will remove the influence of harmful past memories and replace them with positive messages from God, thus reassuring the individual's heart toward the future and preparing him to face it.

The Holy Spirit wants to fill and enrich your life in order to instill in you a dynamic testimony of the abundant Christian life. For Him to do so, you must cooperate by learning the Word of God and keeping it. God blesses those who obey Him, but knowledge always precedes obedience. The psalmist evidently had this in mind when he wrote in the psalm of the happy man, "[Happy] is the man . . . his delight is in the law of the LORD (the Bible) . . . he shall be like a tree planted by the rivers of water, that bringeth forth his fruit in his season; his leaf also shall not wither; and whatsoever he doeth shall prosper" (Ps. 1:1-3).

If you would live the abundant life mentally like a tree whose roots lie near a river of water, then your mind must be refreshed daily with the water of life, the Word of God.

# 11

# Depression and Your Self-Image

"A person's attitude toward himself has a profound influence on his attitude toward God, his family, his friends, his future, and many other significant areas of his life."
*Bill Gothard*
*National Youth Authority*

Every depressed person I have ever counseled has had a problem with self-acceptance. That really is not too profound a statement in view of the fact that almost every human being holds an inadequate image of himself. At some time in his life even the boldest and most self-confident individual battles self-rejection. Although most people regain their self-assurance, none is immune.

In recent years research has produced new concepts called "self-image psychology" that have proved quite helpful to people. Dr. Maxwell Maltz has declared self-image psychology to be the most important discovery of the century. It stems from the idea that each of us is controlled by the mental picture we develop of ourselves.

Two popular expressions from self-image psychology illustrate its basic thesis: "You are what you think

131

you are" and "What other people think of you is not nearly as important as what you think of yourself." Everyone has some image of himself, either good or bad, but whatever that self-image, it affects our behavior, attitudes, productivity, and ultimately our success in life.

Thoughts produce feelings and feelings produce actions; consequently your self-image thoughts definitely affect your actions, negatively or positively.

One who maintains a self-confident image of himself will perform to his maximum ability, but the insecure person who lacks self-confidence will not. This explains why some talented people fail while other mediocre people often succeed.

A person's self-image is not formed by a single event or experience. Instead, it is the culmination of all of life's experiences. Naturally, many subconscious influences produce self-image, including the thousands of victories, failures, frustrations, humiliations, and successes we experience. The influence they have on our self-image depends in large measure on our natural temperament.

Temperament comprises the raw material a person is born with, creating the combination of traits passed on to him by his parents through the genes. It is probably the largest single factor producing personality characteristics. As we shall see in a later chapter, these temperament traits contain both strengths and weaknesses. Whatever your temperament, it will be influenced by your life experiences. If, for example, you were born happy-go-lucky or self-confident by temperament, you may be constrained to develop a defeatist's complex by excessively critical parents who always carp at you or accentuate your ineptitude or failure. Conversely, if you were born with a negative or retiring temperament and are prone to be indecisive and insecure, wise parents can help you avoid a defeatist's attitude by surrounding you with love, acceptance, and encouragement, particularly during the early years of life. Whatever the cause, your personal self-image governs your life! Consider the expression "You are what you think you are." If you think you are ugly or inept, you are. It doesn't matter what you actually are, for what really affects your productivity and actions is what you think you are.

I know a young mother who always commands attention when she walks into a room. Both men and women take a second look at her. When I mentioned this to some associates recently, we all agreed that she was not a beautiful woman, but that something about her drew our attention. As I have come to know her, I find that she enjoys a tremendous amount of self-respect. She always looks her best wherever she goes; she is not overdressed but extremely attractive. She chooses her clothes and accessories with care and exudes the confidence that always exemplifies a dynamic Christian. Neither haughty nor proud, she makes the best use of her assets. I know many of her female friends who are actually better looking women, but they never command that attention. Why? They lack her self-image. It is interesting to note that her self-confidence was not generated by her family, for they have rejected her because of her Christian faith. Only her personal faith in Christ has bestowed upon her a confidence in His ability to enable her to be a dynamic, attractive woman. And she is! )

The two most beautiful women I have ever counseled were severely depressed. To my dismay, neither woman acepted herself. As I looked into their lovely faces, faces which most women would covet, I was reminded that looks alone are irrelevant; how you *think* you look is critical. Neither of these lovely creatures considered herself attractive, so what difference did it make that she was?

The younger of the two was frigid, the slightly older woman a nymphomaniac—yet both shared the same problem. One was so obsessed with the false notion of her inadequate appearance that she could not stand exposure of her body to the opposite sex. The other woman was so obsessed with the inadequacy of her appearance that she drove herself through a series of illicit affairs in an attempt to gain the acceptance she craved. Today both women are well-adjusted, effective Christians, powerful evidence to the stabilizing influence of Jesus Christ in this very needed area of a person's life. It began by recognizing that God forgave and accepted them. That made it easier for them to accept themselves.

## The Big Mistake

Most people make a singular mistake regarding self-image: they allow other people's opinions to influence their view of themselves. Quite to the contrary, what a person thinks of himself will affect what other people think of him. I have seen this illustrated many times while standing at an airline baggage counter. A porter will approach an individual and address him politely and with dignity, whereas he will speak to another with quiet disrespect. Through these contrasting treatments, I have judged that the man who exudes self-confidence and self-acceptance is extended respect by others. You can observe similar episodes in a restaurant as the waiter approaches his customers.

Once a person understands that he creates his public image by his actions and by his impression of himself, he will realize the importance of self-acceptance, which determines whether he will act confidently or with great uncertainty. Be sure of this: if you lack confidence in yourself, so will everyone else.

Here are three good reasons why you should not let others' attitudes influence what you think of yourself:

1) You should accept yourself as God values you, not as other people do.
2) You cannot always judge what people think about you by their appearance or actions, for they may be concentrating on something else entirely.
3) What other people think of you is usually a reflection of your own self-image. If you feel inferior, you emote the feeling of inferiority, and consequently others will look upon you as inferior.

## Four Areas of Self-Acceptance

The Institute of Basic Youth Conflicts, directed by Bill Gothard, has probably helped more people learn the art of self-acceptance with God's help and power than any other training program. The phenomenal success Mr. Gothard achieves is not measured only by the huge crowds that attend his seminars, but also by the thousands of individuals who literally have been transformed by applying the biblical principles he teaches. Most of those who attend his seminars are well-educated in the mental, emotional, and physical areas of life. However, because most of them have been brainwashed by the atheistic, humanistic philosophers of our secular educational system, they noticeably lack spiritual knowledge or reserves. By recognizing the spiritual side of man's nature as described in chapter 6 and by applying the biblical principles Mr. Gothard teaches, these individuals are able to gain self-acceptance and become mature, productive people.

In his seminars Bill Gothard describes four areas in which people must gain self-acceptance. Naturally, it follows that these are the very areas in which most people reject themselves: appearance, abilities, parentage, environment.

(1) *Appearance*—It has been my observation that almost everyone rejects his appearance. Twelve Hollywood actors and actresses were asked the question, "If you could change something about your facial features, what would it be?" The answers ranged anywhere from four to twelve items per person. As incredible as it may seem, these people, admired by millions as the most beautiful or handsome in our society, obviously did not accept themselves. Again we are confronted with this fact: it is not so important what we are, but what we *think* we are.

Rejection of one's appearance is an intensely spiritual problem. Since God is our Creator, we tend to blame Him for our condition. This subconscious and sometimes conscious resentment toward God will keep us from becoming mature Christians. Through the years I have been able to help hundreds of people who lacked the assurance of their salvation to gain that precious emotional blessing. In almost every case I discovered that they lacked assurance in the beginning primarily because they did not like their appearance. According to their standard, they were either too tall, too short, too fat, or too thin. In addition to prescribing the daily reading of the first epistle of John for at least one month, I required them to look in the mirror and thank God for the way they were made. Only by the removal of this resentment toward God for the way they were created could the door be opened for the much needed self-acceptance.

(2) *Abilities*—Except for a very rare number of gifted individuals, most people develop an inadequate view of their abilities, especially when they tend to compare themselves with others. Whether running with a football, riding a motorcycle, or passing a geometry examination, we compete as a way of life. Sooner or later everyone finds someone better than himself, and this may trigger the problem. We regularly tend to make unfair comparisons of our abilities with those of someone else. Just because someone hits sixty home runs a year does not mean that he is a mature person. Many mature and adequate people cannot hit one home run, but they make excellent husbands, fathers, teachers, and people. It is far better to accept the fact that our talents or abilities are conferred by God and that our responsibility in life is to serve and glorify Him (Rev. 4:11). Fulfillment, happiness, and self-acceptance are best found in doing the will of God for one's life.

I regularly discover that the most self-fulfilling use of our talents appears in successfully raising children. Since God's first commandment to man was to be fruitful and multiply and replenish the earth, it follows that the successful fulfillment of that commandment will become a very self-rewarding experience. It must be understood, however, that God was not merely referring to the biological function of begetting children. He had in mind a much longer range view—that of raising those children to be God-conscious Christian young people, taught by their parents the principles of

God and capable of teaching these principles to their own children.

After twenty-five years of dealing with people I do not find that vocational triumphs provide lasting self-acceptance. Instead, many individuals would willingly relinquish the fortune earned during their lifetime if they could reclaim the failure experienced by the son or daughter who was neglected as a child. On the other hand, I know hundreds of happy, contented Christians who feel enriched because their children are a source of pride and satisfaction to them.

Don't think that you must wait until you become a grandparent, however, to achieve this self-recognition. It can be achieved also by spiritual productivity. Those who invest themselves in service for Christ by personally sharing their faith with others usually do not have a lasting problem with self-acceptance. Worthwhile productivity is a great cure-all for self-rejection. That is one reason teenagers are prone to reject themselves —they haven't had time yet to be productive.

(3) *Parentage*—Anyone who is ashamed of his parents will have a serious problem with self-acceptance. Too many young people today hate their parents and bring on themselves the curse of God and the tragic results of harbored animosity. Admittedly, some parents can be decidedly inhuman to their children. As a pastor, I have been called into some unbelievable situations.

Recently I had all I could do to control myself while watching a young mother abuse her young son who looked to be about eighteen months old. While waiting in line at an airline counter, I observed a mother in her mid-twenties rush up to the agent, highly distressed because she was about to miss her plane. At her side was her pajama-clad boy, who, sensing her anxiety, was trying to cling to her side. First she pushed him away with her suitcase, and finally in her exasperation she put her foot in his stomach and shoved him out of the way. The boy fell whimpering to the tile floor as the mother walked off. My final glimpse was of a boy frantically trying to catch up with a fleeing woman, crying as if his heart would break.

It doesn't take a psychiatrist to diagnose what that child will be like as a teenager if he is continually subjected to that kind of treatment. He will certainly become a rebel, always seeking acceptance from others because he has none for himself. His clinging tendency because of continual rejection will gave way to malignant bitterness that will cause him either to reject women and fall a victim to the sin of homosexuality or be cruel to his wife and daughters.

Nothing destroys like bitterness, particularly when it is aimed at one's parents. Having dealt with hundreds of such people, I am convinced that failure to rid oneself of that bitterness will destroy the normal love relationships in life. Only by confessing this spirit of enmity as described in chapter 7 will the individual experience relief. The Bible teaches us, "Cease from anger, and forsake wrath: fret not thyself in any wise to do evil" (Ps. 37:8).

## A Dangerous Fixation

Aside from the spiritual dangers of harboring anger toward one's parents, another tragic result is also undesirable. For years I have noted that young people who hate their parents either grow up to be just like them or marry a partner similar to them. Those who study the function of the brain now explain that such a strange phenomenon originates with the subconscious mind, which always works toward the fulfillment of whatever image we throw upon the screen of our imagination. For example, I have noticed that the young woman raised by an alcoholic father tends to marry an alcoholic. The reason is simple. Thousands of times during her youth a girl has visualized a mental picture of her drunken father and pledged, "I will never marry a man like that!" But her subconscious mind brings her inexorably to the fulfillment of her negative thoughts of disgust or hatred for her father. The same thing happens to the young man whose cruel, angry father mistreated him. Although he insists he will never act like his father, he does. When the child I saw mistreated in the airport grows up and marries, he will probably unite with a woman much like his mother, because all through life his resentment toward her will cause him to project on the screen of his imagination that bitter image, together with the promise, "I will never marry a woman like her." But he will!

## A Healthy Fixation

All of the above mentioned tragedies can be avoided if people would recognize the importance of permitting only those thoughts on the screen of their imagination that are pleasing to God. We cannot always control what thoughts flash onto our imagination screen, but we can regulate those that linger, for those persistent, recurring thoughts activate the subconscious mind, which in turn creates feelings that motivate actions.

Instead of projecting negative images, visualize positive ones. If the young woman had envisioned a wholesome young man embodying Christian principles, instead of her alcoholic father, she would have married that kind of man. Anything else would have violated her mental image. In fact, I know one young woman, the product of an alcoholic father, who rejected a fine Christian lad to marry a man who turned out to be an alcoholic. Why? She fixed upon the wrong kind of mental image in her imagination.

(4) *Environment*—Although highly exaggerated by behaviorists of a past generation, our environment does create a profound effect on our self-acceptance. If a person is embarrassed by his home and family, he will be miserable, and in addition his attitude of shame or rejection will severely mar his self-image out of proportion to the actual circumstances.

To understand that mental attitude toward one's circumstances is far more significant than the material or physical circumstance itself, consider the classic story of the teenage girl who was ashamed of her mother because of hands terribly disfigured by burns. When her father noticed how she avoided being seen in public with her mother, he explained to her in detail how the disfigurement had occurred. When the girl was a baby, her mother had rescued her from falling into an open fireplace. In the process the mother's hands were marred for life. The girl was so ashamed for the heartache she had caused her mother by her selfish attitude that she went to her, took those scarred hands into her own, kissed them, and said through her tears, "Mother, I love you. Can you ever forgive me for the way I have treated you? I don't know how to thank you for all your kindness and love." From then on she was proud to be seen with her mother, and the ugly hands became a badge of honor. What made the difference? Those hands remained just as grotesque as before, but now the daughter's mental attitude toward them had changed.

Some young people have been victimized into a poor self-image by the false notion that second-class people come from second-class living conditions. The products of the ghettos afford good examples. They are trained to think less of themselves because of their ghetto environment. There is nothing new about ghettos; we have always had them. They are simply larger today because of our increased population, and more conspicuous because of recent national attention. During high school I lived in what today would be called a ghetto, but it didn't affect me because no one informed me how terrible it was. I was naive enough to think it was pretty good, so my mental attitude remained positive.

History books are filled with stories of men who have risen from Illinois log cabins to occupy the White House, from ghettos of ignorance to become exemplary educators. A recent survey claimed that the majority of history's successful men have risen above an unfortunate or inadequate environment. The key to your attitude toward your environment involves your acceptance of it. You should at least give thanks for the surroundings which provided you with the life from which to emerge to a better environment, and be grateful for the valuable lessons learned in the process of emerging.

Let us pause here long enough to emphasize that all four areas which influence self-image are affected by a proper spiritual attitude. If you really believe God loves you and has produced you for a special reason, as the Bible teaches, then you can accept with thanksgiving your appearance, abilities, parentage and environment. Once you accept these by faith in God and His Word, you will find it is easy to accept yourself. But if you reject one or more of these areas, you will suffer the miseries that accompany self-rejection. There are undoubtedly other areas of self-acceptance that could be discussed, but these are the main ones.

## The Tragic Results of Rejection

It would be impossible in a small book like this to investigate all the results of self-rejection, for they literally affect everything in a person's life. However, I will offer eight critical consequences of importance.

(1) *Depression*—Resentment that follows the rejection of appearance, abilities, parentage, or environment soon turns into self-pity, which invariably produces depression. This depression will increase in intensity with age unless you learn to accept these areas as instruments of God which He wants to use in your life for His glory. Changes in your environment or life circumstances may provide temporary periods of relief, but unless you modify your thinking pattern of self-pity, you will be chained by the emotional slavery of depression.

(2) *Lack of personal faith in God*—It is impossible to develop a vital and personal faith in God until you learn to accept yourself. Your rejection of God's design of your body, along with His endowment of talents, parents, and environment, are not conducive to the submissive spirit (Eph. 5:21) which is required in a happy, productive Christian. Only by giving thanks by faith for your appearance, talent, parents, and environment can you clear the way for a vital relationship to Him, absolutely essential in ridding yourself of depression.

Most people criticize themselves openly, as we regularly hear in public. But Christians should know better than to censure themselves verbally because they fall short of the standard that God has set before them.

Bill Gothard wisely reminds us that as imperfect as we are, "God is not finished with you yet." As a child of God you are still being molded and fashioned for His divine purposes. Instead of rejecting yourself, according to the Bible you should present yourself to Him and anticipate by faith His ultimate use of your life. Such a spiritual viewpoint will produce a mental attitude conducive to productivity, which in turn will assist self-acceptance.

(3) *Rebellion*—Self-rejection for any reason will kindle the fire of rebellion in your heart toward God and your fellowman, whether parents, boss, life partner, or anyone in authority over you.

We live in a rebellious society. We should not be surprised that we also live in an unhappy society. Think of it! Although we dwell in the lap of luxury with conveniences thought impossible twenty-five years ago, our people are bitter, hostile, and for the most part miserable. This is the typical result of people who reject themselves, for they are prone to lash out at everything and everyone around them.

(4) *Withdrawal*—When a person rejects himself, he finds it difficult to enjoy other people. He tends to be supersensitive to others' attitudes toward his appearance, capabilities, parental background, or environment. Therefore he withdraws so as to avoid conflict and the unhappy feelings it creates. As he retreats, he muses increasingly upon his own needs, feelings, and thoughts. Since he doesn't like himself anyway, he becomes more unhappy.

(5) *Overemphasis on material things*—The rejection of one's self creates an inordinate drive for materialism. This may be characterized by narcissism, an overemphasis on clothes, or the amassing of material goods, none of which produces happiness. It is extremely difficult to convince a young person that the attainment of material possessions does not foster happiness. I can name at least fifteen men worth well over a million dollars who have not found their money a source of happiness, and in some cases wealth has actually destroyed the happiness they enjoyed in less affluent days.

Jesus Christ said, "But seek ye first the kingdom of God, and his righteousness; and all these things shall be added unto you" (Matt. 6:33). By way of contrast to my previous statement, I am familiar with millionaires who are extremely happy. Their money, however, did not bring them happiness. Their primary objective was to serve God, and their material possessions followed in the wake of loyal service.

(6) *Negativism and "failuritis"*—We frequently hear the popular maxim, "Know thyself." Such advice is dangerous to the person who rejects himself, for in practical terms he interprets it to mean "Know thy negative itself." He recollects the past as an amalgamation of failure, affront, insult, and abuse to which he has been subjected. He concludes, "Nothing ever works for me, nothing ever succeeds. I must be doomed to failure!" Since the subconscious mind tends to bring us to the fulfillment of whatever we place on the screen of our imagination, such thinking inevitably produces failure, not because he lacks the potential of success, but because he expects to fail.

(7) *Imitationitis*—The person who rejects himself not only compares himself to others but tries to imitate others. This can be a most harmful practice. Dr. Maxwell Maltz advises, "Remember this, and remember this every day: you will never be happy if you spend your life trying to be someone else. God created you as a unique individual. You have within you an authentic greatness all your own. Use it; don't waste it! You waste it when you try to be someone else for the simple reason you are *not* someone else."[1]

(8) *Limiting God's use of your life*—The sad result of self-rejection is that you keep yourself from being used by God, who fashions a plan for every life. Maximum happiness is achieved in fulfilling that plan, but maximum misery follows in resisting that plan. By rejecting yourself, you not only refrain from using your own natural talents, but you hinder God from injecting His miracle powers into your life. A life of faith is an

[1]Maxwell Maltz, *Psycho-Cybernetics and Self-Fulfillment* (New York: Bantam Books, 1970), p. 96.

exciting life! Most people never experience that kind of living because instead of accepting Jesus Christ's statement, "I am come that they might have life, and that they might have it more abundantly" (John 10:10), they reject themselves and short-circuit the power of God by their unbelief. You will never experience the abundant life until you realize by faith that God is able to bless even *you!*

## Why Most People Tend to Reject Themselves

Anything as universal as self-rejection should have a common cause. Consider the following possibilities:

(1) *Little people in a big world*—We all start out the same way: little people incapable of any productivity. Whether it is a young boy trying to help his father overhaul the family car only to be frustrated with the feeling that his wise father can fix anything whereas he cannot, or the little girl whose clever, experienced mother can bake a cake from scratch while she doesn't know her way around the kitchen, we all share the same problem. Everyone wants to achieve, but we lack the patience to gain the time, training, and experience commensurate with the task.

(2) *Childish ridicule*—No child can grow up without being ridiculed by his peers. For many children, however, such ridicule may teach them to find fault with themselves.

(3) *Being more conscious of one's own mistakes than the mistakes of others*—It has long fascinated me that some perfectionists tend to admire people who are far less capable than themselves. Like David of old, a perfectionist's sins are ever before him. He is, therefore, much more readily confronted with his failures than those of others. In actuality, he becomes far too obsessed with his own faults.

(4) *Critical parents, relatives, teachers, and friends*—Constant criticism is always harmful. Everyone seeks and needs praise, particularly from those he loves most. Unfortunately, the parent who lacks self-esteem often will be overly critical of his children, almost as though he tries to boost his own feelings of importance

by calling attention to their clumsiness and inadequacy. This criticism is regarded by a child as rejection. If his parents reject him, it is easy for him to reject himself.

## The Hallmarks of Self-Acceptance

A mature person is not a perfect person, but one who has learned to accept himself for what he is. That includes both his strengths and weaknesses. He will then try to effect some kind of program to overcome his weaknesses. Without realizing it, this kind of self-acceptance will manifest itself subconsciously in his actions and reactions. As he gradually develops in his spiritual life, he will mature emotionally. Such maturity will be a walking fulfillment of the first two commandments as defined by Jesus Christ which contain the hallmarks of true self-acceptance. ". . . Thou shalt love the Lord thy God with all thy heart, and with all thy soul, and with all thy strength, and with all thy mind; and thy neighbour as thyself" (Luke 10:27).

In addition to these two hallmarks of self-acceptance taught by Christ here there are at least five others. It will be profitable to look briefly at each of them.

(1) *He will love and serve God*—Such an individual will become a submitted Christian, yielded to the will of God. He will not be confused about his identity or constantly driven by ambition to succeed. Instead, his concern with his relationship to God and pleasing Him will overshadow any attempts to gratify himself.

(2) *He will love and accept other people*—A mature person can love others and share life's successes with them. The Bible teaches that we should rejoice with those who rejoice and weep with those who weep. Whereas a mature person will be able to do both, a selfish person can only weep with those who weep. If your neighbor wins a new Cadillac in a drawing, can you honestly rejoice with him? The selfish, immature person will mutter, "Why doesn't something like that ever happen to me?" If the neighbor's wife has died, however, it is not difficult to weep with him without wishing for a similar misfortune. A truly mature person

will love and accept others for themselves and rejoice in their success.

(3) *He will love and accept himself*—Do not fear to love yourself. Christians may be deluded into thinking that any form of self-love is sin, but Jesus did not say, "Do not love yourself." He said, "Love thy neighbor as thyself," aware that self-love in proper perspective is actually essential. Everyone loves himself to some degree, even though harboring thoughts of self-deprecation. However, people too often love themselves more than God or others. Jesus gives ample room for self-love so long as it appears third on your list of priorities.

Proper self-acceptance may be substantiated by the manner in which a person accepts compliments about his work or appearance. Instead of self-consciously brushing the complimenter aside or apologizing for himself, a mature person graciously acknowledges the word of praise. The person who rejects himself becomes flustered and embarrassed, usually extending his embarrassment by uttering something foolish and unnecessary.

(4) *He will exercise responsibility*—A fully mature person is trustworthy, always taking full responsibility for his actions. This is particularly noticeable if something has gone wrong. A self-accepting person will not blame other people for the mistake, for he recognizes that his security and self-acceptance are not contingent on a single experience in life. He is more interested in learning from mistakes than in fixing blame for them. Such maturity betokens good leadership.

(5) *He is emotionally expressive*—A mature person has freedom not only to laugh and to cry if the occasion warrants, but also to respond emotionally to those around him. His joy is not dependent upon people or circumstances, but radiates from within. Ephesians 5:18-21 declares that the Spirit-filled man will have a song in his heart, a thanksgiving spirit, and a submissive attitude. Such an individual will never be depressed.

(6) *He maintains creative flexibility*—A mature

person will readily bend when necessary and readjust his program or schedule when the occasion demands. He is not so intent on having his own way that he becomes insensitive to the needs of others. Many have cheated themselves out of profitable experiences by their resentment toward circumstances over which they have no control. The mature person will be sufficiently relaxed and positive so that when adverse circumstances arise, his creative mind will produce an effective alternative.

(7) *He accepts rebuke, insult, and criticism*—A mature person does not feel threatened when someone corrects him or proposes a better method. Instead, he is appreciative of other people's suggestions and willingly explores better methods for attaining his goals.

## How to Improve Your Self-Image

Since developing a good self-image is so important to overcoming depression, it is worth a few pages of our time to consider workable methods for improvement.

(1) *Develop a personal relationship with God*—Not only is it essential to fill the God-void in yourself by having a personal relationship with Him through His Son Jesus Christ, but it is essential to accept yourself. After filling the God-void in you by receiving Jesus Christ through personal invitation, develop a vital relationship to God in learning about Him as He manifests Himself in His Word. From the first chapter in the Bible, God began to reveal Himself to Adam, Noah, Abraham, and others by the use of different names (the word "name" literally means "nature"). Consequently, each time God added a new name for Himself in the Old Testament, He disclosed a new aspect of His nature that was needed by His children at that point. Like Abraham, the more we learn about God, the more we grow to love Him and the easier it becomes to trust ourselves to Him.

There is only one way to learn about God: read, hear, study, meditate, and memorize what He teaches about Himself in the Bible. Secular man, fully ignorant of God, has a strong problem with self-rejection; only by gaining knowledge of God as revealed in His Word can one develop the ability to accept himself. As Colossians 3:16, 17 enjoins us, "Let the word of Christ dwell in you richly in all wisdom; teaching and admonishing one another in psalms and hymns and spiritual songs, singing with grace in your hearts to the Lord. And whatsoever ye do in word or deed, do all in the name of the Lord Jesus, giving thanks to God and the Father by him." If the Word of God dwells in you richly, you will naturally find peace toward God, yourself, and your fellowman.

(2) *Accept yourself as a creature of God*—The Bible tells us that we are "fearfully and wonderfully made." Since God formed you for His own purposes, you must accept yourself for the fulfillment of these purposes. By looking to Him for guidance, power, and instruction, you link yourself with the omnipotent power of God. If you are a Christian, learn to accept yourself by starting to thank Him for who you are as a member of His divine family.

The importance of this step in self-acceptance can be illustrated in the life of a young woman who spoke to me after a seminar recently. Approximately twenty-two years of age, she sported dowdy-looking corduroy trousers and long, stringy hair. Indicating that she had an irrepressible habit of itching her scalp on one side of her head until she was bald in that spot, she swept back a portion of her tresses to reveal the bald spot. She then related that her father had sent her to the best dematologist in the city, but he could find nothing organically wrong. She had taken several kinds of tranquilizers and spent a few sessions with psychiatrists, but nothing seemed to improve her condition. When I probed for the problem of self-acceptance, she hung her head and acknowledged that she did not like her appearance. I immediately suggested two courses of action: (1) Look yourself squarely in the mirror and thank God for your appearance (she really wasn't unattractive but obviously thought she was); (2) Visit a beauty parlor and have your hair fashioned in such a way that it protects the bald spot and prevents you from itching your scalp without ruining the hairdo. Within six weeks I received word from her that little hairs had begun to grow on the bald spot. This young woman had so convinced herself she was unsightly that she had subconsciously proceeded to destroy her minimal attractiveness by rubbing herself bald and dressing in a most uncomplimentary manner.

A person's appearance is quite often an index of self-acceptance. If he feels inadequate, slovenly, and downcast, he will wear clothes that exhibit those feelings. If, however, he possesses an adequate supply of self-acceptance, he will dress commensurate with his vocation, environment, and resources. I am further inclined to believe that the modern tendency toward dowdiness and unladylike or ungentlemanly clothes worn by high school and college students will perpetuate their actual feelings of self-rejection. What they interpret to be a broadside at the establishment is often little more than an expression of inadequacy and self-disapproval. Naturally, it is dangerous to generalize here, for some prefer casual clothes because they are more comfortable, but it should not be forgotten that we gain a certain psychological comfort in being well-dressed when the occasion calls for it. A person's tastes in style may change with age and maturity, but such changes often signal responses to self-acceptance.

(3) *Learn how to cope with guilt feelings*—One commonly finds self-rejecting people highly discouraged with themselves because of minor blunders, but their frustration is usually well out of proportion to the failure, and they seem to forget that everyone fails himself, society, and God at times. Unfortunately, modern psychology has done its best to explain away guilt by blaming it on religion rather than administering a remedy for it.

Some years ago a doctor friend treating me for laryngitis took advantage of my inoperative voice to inform me rather pointedly that in his opinion ministers had "done more harm to more people than any other known profession." He went on to explain that during his internship in a mental institution, he found that "ninety-five percent of the patients were there be cause of religiously induced guilt complexes." "Doctor, you couldn't be more in error," I whispered. "People feel guilty because they *are* guilty!" The Bible teaches what modern psychology tends to reject: that man is not a conscience-free animal who can sin with impunity, but a living soul whose conscience either accuses or excuses him (Rom. 2:15).

To enjoy good mental health and self-acceptance, conscience must not be ignored! Instead of expecting a psychiatrist to explain away one's pangs of conscience, an individual needs to face his sins and appropriate God's forgiveness. For that reason God has sent the *good news* that "Christ Jesus came into the world to save sinners" (1 Tim. 1:15).

The New Testament is filled with this good news that man can receive forgiveness from God and deliverance from the tyranny of his guilty conscience. But forgiveness begins with personal acknowledgment of sin, for the Bible teaches that "all have sinned, and come short of the glory of God" (Rom. 3.23). Having confessed his sin, man needs to accept God's judgment upon sin in His own Son on Calvary's cross and to recognize that "the blood of Jesus Christ his Son cleanseth us from all sin" (1 John 1:7). The meaning of the verse is that actually God "keeps on cleansing" us from our sin.

Having once gained pardon for his sin, man should thank God by faith for that forgiveness. The sense of release from the tyranny of a guilty conscience will motivate him to desire a life more pleasing to God. When, however, he again falls short of the standard of God, he should understand that he can once more avail himself of this forgiveness. A clear conscience is essential to adequate self-acceptance, but it is a gift of God, *not* a work of man.

Perfectionists in particular struggle with a giant conscience, who bullies them unmercifully because they fail to live up to their standards. They need to learn that if God, who is perfect, can forgive their sins, certainly they and their fellowmen, who throughout life "fall short of the glory of God," should forgive themselves.

(4) *Praise and thank God for your successes*—It is never healthy to let one's mind linger over negative matters, for such rumination fosters griping and self-pity, which in turn produces depression. Instead, it is therapeutic to thank God for His blessings. I have found this particularly helpful in marriage counseling when one member of the family indicates he has lost his love for his partner. I encourage him to list ten things about his partner that he values, then thank God verbally each day for these ten attributes and refuse the temptation to think negatively. It is amazing to watch the renewal of love, even in one who has convinced himself that it is impossible to regain that original romantic response.

Recently in a counseling situation I met a very beautiful but insecure, frigid, and tense wife. It quickly became obvious to me that this lovely creature had nourished the sin of self-rejection even before she married her dynamic, perfectionist husband. Every night when he came home from a work, he treated her with cold contempt and disdain because nothing she did pleased him, and like most men, he did not understand a woman's unusual ability to read a man's spirit. Her failure to satisfy him and her painful consciousness of his rejection severely compounded her self-rejection. And the more she rejected herself, the less motivated she became to attempt to please him. Her situation turned into a vicious cycle.

When I counseled with her husband he was amazed when I explained that he was the key to his wife's condition. I then urged him to select ten positive qualities he found in his wife and thank God for them twice every day, in the morning and on the way home from work. Before long he reported that she became more affectionate and showed signs of self-respect and motivation, all of which signaled improved self-acceptance. Recently I asked him if he had memorized his list by this time. He replied with a smile, "I not only have it memorized, but I'm finding new things in her to be grateful for every day."

Thanksgiving begets thanksgiving. Once you develop a thinking pattern of thanksgiving for the Lord, yourself, loved ones, famliy, job, ad infinitum, you will find it easy to be grateful. Thankful people cannot become depressed.

(5) *Face the future with excited anticipation*—Everyone reading this book has a future, but more important than the details of that future is your attitude toward it. In fact, many authorities stress that your expectations for the future help to create your future.

The Christian has no cause to dread the future. Repeatedly Jesus admonished His disciples for the benefit of all succeeding generations of Christians, "Be of good cheer . . . Go, and lo, I am with you alway, even unto the end of the age." Since Jesus Christ is with us now and will accompany us in the future, we have no adequate reason to dread what it may hold.

Happy is the Christian who develops the habit of greeting each day with an attitude of expectation, eager to appropriate God's blessing and provision. Recently I shared a motel room with a Spirit-filled minister who is well-known for his spontaneous spirit of rejoicing and praise. Our alarm went off at 6:10 A.M. Though the sun was shrouded by a bleak and wintry cloud layer, my friend shut off the alarm and exclaimed aloud, "Good morning, world! Thank You, Jesus for this new and exciting day!" I couldn't help but conclude that he had captured what the psalmist meant when he said, "This is the day which the LORD hath made: we will rejoice and be glad in it" (Ps. 118:24). People who approach life daily with this mental attitude do not face the problem of depression.

# 12

# Depression and Your Temperament

As various attempts have been made to explain man's behavior, numerous theories have been generated. The ancients emphasized man's inherited traits as the cause for his actions. Freud and his followers blamed man's environment and childhood experiences for his behavior. Actually, both contribute to our conduct, but our inherited temperament influences us most.

Through the genes at conception, man inherits from his parents and grandparents his entire nature, including the color of his hair, eyes, body structure, talents, and, of course, his temperament. That temperament acts as the most powerful single influence on his behavior, for it is the cause of his spontaneous actions and reactions. Occasionally some of the brainwashed victims of modern psychology try to accentuate the significance of "learned behavior," but I find that suggestion rather puzzling. Our four children were all raised in the same basic home environment and were subjected to the same training principles, but they are as different as night and day! Something dissimilar in their inherited ingredients must have caused that. Our boys' closet was always a case in point. One side was orderly and neat, the other like the aftermath of a tornado. Our girls were equally different. One loved to dress in "grubbies" and to this day prefers casual clothes for everyday wear. The other girl, before she was three years old, showed a strong preference for dress-up styles and coordinated outfits. Those and a host of other differences appeared in their lives long before we had time to teach such things.

At this writing our first grandchild is nine months old. Before she could crawl, I detected the same traits of strong will and dogged determination I have observed in both her parents. The reason should be obvious! She inherited certain temperament traits that spark her actions and reactions.

## The Four Basic Temperaments

Made up of the traits we inherit at conception, temperament is influenced later by childhood training, education, life experiences, environment, and both human and spiritual motivation.

The best theory of temperament was proposed by Hippocrates 2400 years ago. He suggested that people fit into four basic categories: the sanguine super-extrovert salesman, the choleric extrovertish strong-willed leader, the melancholy introvert perfectionist, and the phlegmatic super-introvert passivist. Although variations have been suggested, this theory is disseminated today very similar to its original form. Perhaps the key addition is that no one fits perfectly into *one* of Hippocrates' molds, for people tend to represent a blend of two or more of these temperaments. This seems a reasonable corollary since they show physical characteristics of both the mother and father.

Most people tend to be predominantly one temperament with slight traits of another. It is not uncommon for a person to be 80% sanguine and 20% phlegmatic, or 70% choleric and 30% melancholic. There is no end of variations and percentages these traits may produce; one man I tested proved to be about 60% sanguine, 20% melancholy, and 20% phlegmatic.

## Temperament and Transformed Temperaments

The analysis of human temperament involves one of the most fascinating subjects I have ever studied.

And although it is tempting to launch into a comprehensive discussion of it here, in the interest of space I am forced to resist. Instead, I suggest you read my books entitled *Spirit-Controlled Temperament* and *Transformed Temperament** for a full presentation of the subject. In this book we will touch on the subject of temperament only as it relates to the problem of depression.

## The Sanguine and Depression

The sanguine temperament breeds a warm, friendly, and outgoing person who draws people to himself like a magnet. He is a good talker, a happy-go-lucky optimist, the "life of the party." Though generous and compassionate, responsive to his surroundings and to the moods or feelings of others, like the other temperaments he features some natural weaknesses. He is often weak-willed, emotionally unstable and explosive, restless and egotistical. Voted "most likely to succeed" in his youth, he rarely measures up to expectations. He has great difficulty following through on details and is almost never quiet. Beneath his bold exterior he is often insecure and fearful. Sanguines make good salesmen, speakers, actors, and sometimes leaders.

A sanguine is rarely depressed when in the company of others. He is such a response-oriented person that the sight of another individual usually lifts his spirits and brings a smile to his face. Whatever periods of depression he does experience almost invariably commence when he is alone.

The most pleasant characteristic of a sanguine is his ability to enjoy the present. He does not look back on unhappy experiences in his past, and he never worries about the unknown future. A delightful sanguine friend of mine affords a classic example. While traveling across the country, he commented on the many people who approached me for counseling due to depression. Spontaneously he exclaimed, "You know, I've never had much trouble with depression; I guess it's

*Published by Tyndale House Publishers, Wheaton, Illinois.

because God has been so good to me. Actually, I can't remember ever having any real problems or difficulties in life." His statement really astonished me, for I knew the man well. I was forced to recall that he failed to finish high school until he was almost forty years of age because he ran away from home and joined the Merchant Marines. While in the service he married, and after two children were born, one of them died of a rather strange and rare disease. This caused some bitterness on the part of his wife, who after several unhappy years divorced him and remarried. At the time my friend made his statement, he had been single for six years. Only a sanguine could recollect that type of life and state, "I've never really had any problems in life." But there would be much less depression if all temperaments could think that way.

Many undisciplined sanguines experience depression during the fourth or fifth decade of life. Their lack of discipline and weakness of will has usually made them rather unproductive, much to their own chagrin and self-disappointment. They are also prone to obesity by this time because of their inability to refuse fattening desserts and other delicacies. This lowers their self-esteem and heightens their tendency toward depression. Although they usually go through the motions of responding happily to other people, their tendency toward mild depression will increase. One writer likened them to Peter Pan—they wish never to grow up. Although they are well-liked and attractive, they are undependable and without real substance.

As these charming sanguines who often act like overgrown children become aware of their own shallowness, their insecurities are heightened. They become defensive, sensitive to slights or criticism, almost obsessed with others' opinions of them. It is not uncommon for them to become depressed at this point by engaging in self-pity. They may even blame their parents for indulging them so much in childhood that they never developed self-discipline, but it is very difficult for them to blame themselves, confess their sin, and seek the filling of the Holy Spirit for the strength of character they so desperately need.

If they do not face their problem realistically and learn to walk in the Spirit, they will fluctuate up and down between depression and happiness for a time until, in some childlike way, they make the mental adjustment and then go through life fixed in a playful position far beneath their level of potential.

The Spirit-filled sanguine is different! The Holy Spirit not only convicts him of his self-pitying thought patterns as sin, but guides him to those areas of productivity that make it easier for him to accept and appreciate himself. When a sanguine is filled with the Spirit, like the Apostle Peter in the Book of Acts, he becomes a productive and effective person, untroubled by depression.

## The Choleric Temperament and Depression

The choleric temperament produces a practical activist. He is strong-willed, a natural leader, and very optimistic. His brain is filled with ideas, projects, or objectives, and he usually sees them through. Like Mr. Sanguine he is extrovertish, but not nearly so intense. Although very productive in life, he reflects serious natural weaknesses. He is self-sufficient, impetuous, and hot-tempered, and he tends to be harsh or cruel. In fact, no one can be as cutting and sarcastic as a choleric. He makes a good supervisor, general, builder, crusader, politician, or organizer, but is not usually able to do precise detail work.

The choleric rarely becomes depressed, primarily because his active, goal-conscious mind keeps him so motivated that he projects fourteen different programs simultaneously. If one of them proves baffling or frustrating, his disappointment is short-lived and he quickly pursues a fresh challenge. Cholerics are happy when busy, and thus they have little time to be depressed. Their primary frustration in life is that there are not enough hours in the day to engage in their endless supply of goals and objectives.

The rejection or insults that often set other temperaments off into periods of depression never faze a choleric. He is so thick-skinned, self-sufficient, and independent by nature that he rarely feels the need for other people. Instead of feeling sorry for himself when alone, he spends the time originating new plans.

Emotionally he is the most underdeveloped of all the temperaments. For that reason he usually experiences very slight mood changes. Although he quickly becomes angry, he rarely indulges in self-pity. Instead, he explodes all over everyone else. Because he is so insensitive to others' opinions of him, he is not vulnerable to depression occasioned by people. If a choleric ever battles depression, it will come as a result of frustration or retreat.

By the time a choleric has reached the fourth or fifth decade of life, his activity-prone brain can often create a mental activity syndrome that makes his thoughts cancel or short-circuit each other, much like an overloaded switchboard. This tendency was noted in our chapter on the causes of depression. As a Christian, the choleric must learn to rest in the Lord and commit his way to Him. An indomitable will and spirit of self-sufficiency often causes him to be a useless, unproductive Christian because he insists on doing everything in the flesh instead of the Spirit. If he does successfully promote Christian activities, his pride makes him spiritually myopic and he fails to discern his carnal motivation.

The peace of the Holy Spirit that passes all understanding will modulate his thinking pattern, causing him to concentrate on the Lord first and then on the task. He must learn that God's program does not depend on him; rather, he needs to depend on God. He must further recognize that fulfilling the work of God is not enough; he must do it in the power of the Spirit. As the Bible says, "Not by might, nor by power, but by my Spirit, saith the LORD of hosts" (Zech. 4:6). The Apostle Paul, possibly the best illustration of a Spirit-filled choleric used of God, had learned this well, for he said, ". . . when I am weak, then am I strong" (2 Cor. 12:10).

The flesh-filled choleric Christian can become depressed until he realizes this principle, because he gets frustrated by the lack of spiritual results from his hard-driving, fleshly efforts. Instead of blaming himself for his carnal, self-willed spirit, he may swell up in self-pity and withdraw from his church activities. His carnal spirit is often easily discerned by others in the congregation, and thus he may be bypassed when officers are elected. "I don't understand," he complains. "Isn't my hard work sufficient proof of my devotion to Christ?" Happy is the choleric who learns with James to say, ". . . If the Lord will, we shall live, and do this, or that" (James 4:15). If he seeks the priorities of the will of God through the leading of the Holy Spirit in his life, he will not only be more productive but also more composed. When once he comprehends that walking in the Spirit is the secret to spiritual productivity, he will gain consistency in his Christian life.

Another period of life during which a choleric is vulnerable to depression is retirement. Though he usually does not retire until age seventy or later, he must program into his thinking some added form of productivity or give way to depression.

A former business executive was forced to retire at sixty-five. Within six months he went in to see his pastor in a state of depression. It did not take the minister long to perceive that the unproductive inactivity of retirement was the culprit. In addition, of course, the executive was indulging in the sin of self-pity that laments, "My life is over, the period of my productivity is past, I am no longer good for anything." The pastor was leading a very dynamic church much in need of a businessman to coordinate and direct the business affairs. He challenged this man to be a $1.00 a year Christian worker. Today that church rates among the most efficient in the nation, and the energetic choleric business manager is thoroughly enjoying his retirement.

The ability of the Holy Spirit to literally transform a choleric tendency to depression is illustrated superbly in the life of the Apostle Paul. If ever a man was an illustration of choleric temperament, it was Saul of

Tarsus before he became a Christian. After his conversion, his indomitable choleric will directed by the Holy Spirit surged forward throughout the Book of Acts. His response to confinement offers a classic illustration of depressing circumstances overcome through the invasion of man's spiritual nature by the Holy Spirit. Confined to the cold, clammy Mamertine Prison in Rome for preaching the Gospel, he manifested not one sign of self-pity. Instead, this dynamic Christian took advantage of the opportunity to share his faith personally with every new Roman soldier assigned to him as a guard. So many of these men were converted that he addressed the church of Rome, "All the saints salute you, chiefly they that are of Caesar's household" (Phil. 4:22). In addition, from this prison he penned the prison epistles, including the epistle of joy called the letter to the Philippians, in which he stated, "I have learned, in whatsoever state I am, therewith to be content" (Phil. 4:11). Spirit-filled cholerics will never become depressed.

## The Melancholy Temperament and Depression

The richest of all temperaments is the melancholy. Rich not only in gifts and esthetic appreciation, it has the capacity to experience the entire spectrum of emotional mood fluctuations. In addition, it is also rich in emotional weaknesses, particularly in the tendency to be depressed. Some of the world's greatest geniuses have been gifted melancholics who squandered their talent in the slough of despondency, becoming apathetic and unproductive. This is so much in evidence that the ancients frequently used the words melancholy and depression interchangeably.

The melancholy is usually the most talented of all temperaments. A natural perfectionist, very sensitive and appreciative of the fine arts, he is analytical and self-sacrificing. As a rule he is not outgoing by nature and rarely pushes himself forward, but he makes a very faithful friend. However, he tends to be moody, critical, pessimistic, and self-centered. The world's great artists, composers, philosophers, inventors, and theoreticians have usually been melancholies.

Although everyone is vulnerable to his own mental thinking pattern, none is more responsive than the melancholy. Among his other creative gifts, he harbors the great ability to suggest images to the screen of his imagination—probably in living color with stereophonic sound. Because melancholies are moody by nature, they may regard their moods as spontaneous, but it has been learned that moods result directly from thinking patterns. If a melancholy guards his thought processes and refuses to indulge in the mental sins of anger, resentment, self-persecution, and self-pity, he will not yield to his predisposition toward depression.

The powerful influence of the mind on our moods can easily be illustrated by an experience I had with my sons when they were growing up. One Sunday night as they were going to bed we reminded them, as millions of children are faithfully reminded by loving parents, "Don't forget—tomorrow you have to get up early and go to school." In unison they sang, "Do we have to go to school tomorrow?" Assuring them that this was a necessary part of their lives and accepting their grumbling with customary parental long-suffering, I sent them off to bed. Needless to say, Monday morning they woke up in a sour mood. I sincerely hated to foist them off on their schoolteacher that day.

Next week the same boys were lying in the same bed at night. As I tucked them in I admonished, "Don't forget, you've got to get up early tomorrow because we're heading for Disneyland!" You can imagine the happy chorus that greeted my announcement. The next morning both boys bolted out of bed, excited and expectant, as they anticipated the thrilling trip ahead. As I sat at the breakfast table that morning, I contemplated the difference in moods within just one week. Their metabolism seemed to function better, their eyes were clearer, their faces shinier, the whole world looked better *because they reflected an improved mental attitude*. The melancholy who recognizes the power of the subconscious mind to influence his moods will seek the power of the Holy Spirit to orient his thinking patterns positively.

It is hard to select one period in life that a melancholy finds more depressing than another. Usually his depressions become apparent in early childhood; unless he is spiritually motivated by the power of God, they tend to follow him all his life. Because he is supersensitive and self-centered, he reads things into every activity, at times becoming almost obsessed with the idea that people don't like him or that they are laughing at him.

One day the business manager of Christian Heritage College, my wife (who is the Registrar), and I were having lunch together in a restaurant. Suddenly a melancholy college-age man with a gaunt look on his face appeared at the edge of our table and asked, "Pardon me, but may I ask you folks if you were laughing at me?" Naturally we were shocked into silence. Finally I explained, "Young man, I don't think we've ever seen you before in our lives." With that he excused himself and walked away. Reflecting on the incident, we concluded that during our laughter and conversation we must have looked in his direction, which gave that troubled young man the impression that we were laughing at this expense. Equally as substantial are many of the depression-causing events in the life of the average melancholy.

## Melancholy Perfectionists

Melancholies often are easily depressed because they are perfectionists. Most people could profit by having more perfectionist tendencies, but the true perfectionist is made miserable by them. In the first place, he measures himself by his own arbitrary standard of perfection and gets discouraged with himself when he falls short of that standard. The fact that his standard is usually so high that neither he nor anyone else could live by it rarely occurs to him. Instead, he insists that his criterion for perfection is "realistic."

In addition to perfectionism he also is very conscientious and prides himself on being "dependable" and "accurate." Naturally, all of his friends fall short of this standard, so it is not uncommon for him to become depressed about himself and his associates. Very rigid and inflexible, he finds it difficult to tolerate the slightest deviation from what he considers to be the measure of excellence.

Such perfectionist-prone melancholies can love their children dearly while at the same time becoming depressed by them. Children are notoriously disorganized and unpredictable; they follow their own schedules and insist on acting like children. A rigid melancholy parent finds it difficult to cope with such unpredictability and consequently may experience depression. Sometimes a melancholy mother may become ambivalent toward her own children, loving them intensely while at the same time being filled with anger and bitterness at them. The carefree, happy-go-lucky little tyke who insists on trekking across the clean kitchen floor with his wet rubbers can be a source of irritation to any mother, particularly to a melancholy. Before she was married, she probably could not retire for the night until her shoes were lined up properly and the bathroom was in perfect order. Children automatically change that, but perfectionists find it difficult to cope with such change; consequently, depression is their outlet. They become angered at the lack of perfection in others and indulge in self-pity because they are the only ones striving for lofty goals. Such thought patterns invariably produce depression.

In fairness to melancholy people, they are as critical of themselves as they are of others. Consequently, they tend to develop an inadequate view of themselves. From early childhood they construct a disparaging self-image on the screen of their imagination. As they get older, unlike some of the other temperaments who learn to accept themselves, they tend to reject themselves even more. Consequently their periods of depression increase. If they were permitted to verbalize their criticisms in childhood, they are apt to be verbally critical in adulthood. Each time they indulge in oral criticism, they only embed the spirit of criticism more deeply in their mind, and critics are never happy people!

One day I had an opportunity to see this principle in action. As I submitted to an airport examination before boarding a plane, the security officer began to criticize the individuals who flew on that airline as "slovenly, inconsiderate, disorganized and ungrateful people." I took it just about as long as I could, but finally, looking at him with a big smile (I find one can say almost anything if he smiles) I observed, "You must be an unhappy man!" He looked at me rather startled and replied, "Why do you say that?" "Because you're so critical. I've never met a happy person who is a critical person." After inspecting my baggage, he said, "Thank you, sir, I needed that." To my amazement he turned to the next customer and said, "Hello, how are you? So glad to have you on our airline." I don't know how long he will profit by that experience, but I am certain that he has the capability of making himself happy or miserable in direct proportion to the way in which he thinks and talks to people.

Not only are melancholy people rigid perfectionists and conscientious individuals, but they possess a low threshold of anxiety and tension. The American way of life is not conducive to happiness for such people. We live in a hyperactivity-prone, choleric society, as Dr. Paul Tournier verifies in a chapter on temperament in his book entitled *The Healing of Persons*. It seems that western civilization, where the Gospel of Christ has had its most profound influence, reflects a highly choleric population. This would be characteristic of the Teutonic or Nordic race, whose people tend to represent a high percentage of choleric temperament. Such individuals settled in Scandinavia, Germany, parts of France, Ireland, and England, the very countries producing most of the American settlers. Although it would be difficult to prove, it would seem that the most courageous, hearty, and choleric members of Europe came over to settle this country. Consequently, their progeny would include a high level of choleric, activity-prone citizens, which may account for our industrialized, fast-moving, high-pressure environment. Such an atmosphere is not the best for a melancholy, for he is not interested in achieving massive production, but perfection and quality. It is not uncommon to hear a melancholy professional man complain, "We just don't have time to be accurate anymore."

This may explain why so many of the hippy or "freak" people "drop out" of the mainstream of society today. Rejecting its mad pace and witnessing its lack of perfection through the eyes of idealism, they seek a more passive culture. This may be one reason some of them will speak favorably about a governmental system that has totally enslaved people into passivity in contrast to the free enterprise system, which they think has enslaved people to activity.

I have repeatedly observed that many of the young people who have "copped out" of our society are very sensitive, gifted, idealistic young people indulging in escape rather than making an honest attempt to alter society. Dr. Tournier notes that some of the Indian or Oriental cultures place a higher priority on the mystic or passive individual. Thus Mahatma Gandhi, whose fastings were symbolic of passive resistance, became a national hero. By contrast, in the western world the dynamic, productive choleric is the hero. Whatever its cause, the frantic pace we live in today contributes heavily to the melancholy's tendency toward depression.

## Self-Sacrifice and Persecution-Prone

Two characteristics of the melancholy which mutually short-circuit each other are his natural desire to be self-sacrificing and his self-persecution tendency. Unless he is careful, this conflict will likely make a martyr out of him. Ordinarily he chooses the most difficult and trying location to ply his vocation. When others seem to be more successful or gain more renown, instead of facing realistically the fact that he has chosen the path of self-sacrifice he indulges in self-pity because his journey winds uphill and leads through arduous straits.

The determination of a melancholy to gripe and criticize merely compounds his negative thinking and ultimately brings him to despair. For that reason 1 Thessalonians 5:18 can come to his rescue! If he painstakingly and consistently follows its formula, he will never become depressed. *"In every thing give thanks: for this is the will of God in Christ Jesus concerning you."*

## Melancholy Creativity

Fortunately for the melancholy, he possesses an unusual creative ability to project all kinds of images on the screen of his imagination. Once he fully realizes that his feelings are the direct result of constructing wholesome mental images of himself and his circumstances, he is well on the road to recovery and prevention of future bouts of depression. Melancholy people risk depression primarily because of the continual misuse of their creative imagination. That is, on the imagination screen of their mind they project negativism, self-pity, helplessness, and despair. Once they realize that their creative suggestions can either work for or against them, they can carefully project only those images that are pleasing to God. Such thoughts will lift their spirits, stabilize their moods, and help them to avoid depression.

## The Phlegmatic and Depression

The easygoing, never-get-upset "nice guy" is the phlegmatic. In addition to featuring a calm and likable disposition, Mr. Phlegmatic is a cheerful fellow who works well with other people, an efficient, conservative, dependable, witty person with a practical turn of mind. Since he is quite introvertish, as a rule, his weaknesses, like his strengths, are not as readily perceptible as those of other temperaments. His most obvious weakness is lack of motivation. He can ignore work graciously and is prone to be stubborn, stingy, and indecisive. His ability to look at life through the eyes of a spectator may generate a tendency to avoid "getting involved" with anything. Phlegmatics make good diplomats since they are natural peacemakers. Many are teachers, doctors, scientists, comedians, and magazine and book editors. When externally motivated, they make very capable leaders.

As a general rule, a phlegmatic person is not easily depressed. His unique sense of humor signals a happy outlook on life, and rarely does he reflect much mood fluctuation. It is possible to know a phlegmatic all his life and never see him truly angry, for no matter what the occasion, he tends to mentally excuse the person who has offended, injured or rejected him. His ability to adjust to unpleasant circumstances is unbelievable to the other three temperaments, which find it easy to gripe or criticize mentally and verbally.

If a phlegmatic ever does experience depression, it is usually aimed at his own lack of aggressiveness. Many times his practical, capable mind devises a suitable plan of action for a given set of circumstances, but because of his passive inclination, or his fear of being criticized by others, he keeps it to himself. Consequently, driven by family or other group pressure, he may find himself pursuing a plan inferior to his own. This can produce irritation which, when followed by self-pity, will make him depressed. Fortunately, his depression is short-lived most of the time, for in a brief time one of those amazingly interesting characters called a human being comes along to amuse and entertain him.

At one critical period in life the phlegmatic is most vulnerable to depression. During the fifth or sixth decade he often becomes aware that the other temperaments have passed him by vocationally, spiritually, and in every other way. While he was passively watching the game of life as a spectator, his more aggressive friends were stepping through the doors of opportunity. His security-mindedness has checked him from attending upon daring adventures in life, and thus his existence may seem rather stale to him during this period. If he indulges in self-pity, he will definitely become depressed.

Instead of blaming his fear or indolence, he finds it much easier to reproach "society" or "the breaks" or "my luck." Such a person should learn from the Lord Jesus early in life to attempt great things for God, for Christ said, "According to your faith be it unto you!" (Matt. 9:29).

## Marital Frustration—Phlegmatic Depression

Phlegmatics usually make good marriage partners. They are relatively easy to live with, and even though they are quite selfish, they usually give in during controversy because they "just don't like turmoil." But capitulating against one's will can lead to bitterness and results in self-pity—followed by depression. The only lasting remedy for a phlegmatic (or any temperament) is to walk in the Spirit and learn to submit "one to another in the fear of God" (Eph. 5:21). He must learn to surrender his rights to God and his partner and genuinely seek his partner's happiness. When a person enters marriage "for what I can get out of it," he will always be disappointed. However, when he determines to insure his partner's happiness, his own is guaranteed. Paul said, "Whatsoever a man soweth, that shall he also reap." I have yet to find a miserable, unhappy partner who genuinely set out to bring joy into the life of his spouse.

Surrender in marriage, when discharged in the right spirit, has an amazing effect on a partner, improving objectivity, removing competition and inspiring the desire to reciprocate kindness. Many times it has the effect of "heaping coals of fire" on a spouse's head, for after getting his own way in a given situation, the spouse may be so overcome by guilt that he will be less aggressive or demanding the next time. But the crucial question is: Does the one surrendering do so joyfully or in self-pity? The answer determines whether or not the surrender is followed by depression.

A phlegmatic person must be unusually vigilant at

this point, for he too frequently avoids conflict by giving in—while resenting it mentally. Self-pitying thoughts generally follow in the wake of resentment, and the consequent depression will subvert emotional stability.

## Opposites Attract Each Other

Family Life Seminar audiences laugh uproariously at some of my illustrations of opposites attracting each other in marriage. Their merriment is cut short, however, when they discover the grim truth that one's weaknesses inevitably collide with his partner's strengths in the test tube of marriage. Unless couples learn to work toward adjusting to their partner's traits and habits, they are headed for conflict.

The captivating strengths that you found so alluring in your fiancé before marriage may be effaced by the disagreeable appearance of corresponding weaknesses afterward. Somehow that problem was not anticipated. You may have sensed that your partner's strengths corresponded to your weaknesses, which attracted you in the first place, but satisfaction gives place to alarm when you discover that your partner's weaknesses relate to an area of your strength. Ah, there's the rub! It is so easy to look contemptuously and disdainfully upon another person's weakness— when it falls in an area of your strength!

## Phlegmatics Don't Always Marry Cholerics!

Although it is usually dangerous to generalize about people, I have repeatedly observed that like temperaments do not marry. Of the 428 couples whose marital knots I have tied, to my knowledge, none were temperament twins. This is particularly true of phlegmatics, who generally marry cholerics. But such a union can produce its own unique predisposition to depression.

If the choleric is the wife, the phlegmatic husband may face depression because "I can't stand that woman always pressuring me!" What seemed before marriage to be the woman's "dynamic leadership and practicality" becomes bossy, domineering autocracy after marriage. By contrast, the choleric wife discovers that the "kind, gentle, patient" boy friend melts into a "weak, unmotivating, unchallenging, humdrum" husband. The harassed phlegmatic husband will rarely stand up for his convictions against his more forceful mate—and experiences depression because of his failure to "assert his manhood," and also because of his self-pitying thought patterns.

The offended and often criticized phlegmatic wife of a choleric often indulges in self-pity because she can do nothing to please her husband. She is "too slow, too unmotivated and too unchallenging." His vented wrath strips her of any self-image she brought into the marriage, and by the time his sarcastic outbursts have left her battered and bowed a few times, she adds "depression" to her list of undesirable characteristics.

Yes, phlegmatics can get depressed. They may resist depression a litle longer than other temperaments, but neglect of their spiritual resources will make them prey to its snare.

## The Remedy for Temperament Weakness

God has a thrilling plan for overcoming all temperament weaknesses—even depression. In Ephesians 5:18 He designates it as being continually "filled with the Spirit." As we shall point out in a future chapter, the filling of the Holy Spirit produces three great emotional characteristics:

1) A song in your heart (Eph. 5:19)
2) A thanksgiving mental attitude (Eph. 5:20)
3) A submissive spirit (Eph. 5:21)

It is impossible to be depressed when you realize all three of these emotions. The filling of the Spirit, then, is the obvious remedy for emotional depression.

## Is All Depression Caused by Self-Pity?

Almost every time I speak on depression, someone with a sad look on his face asks, "Aren't there any exceptions? Surely some depression must be caused organically." We have been so conditioned to blaming our behavior on other people or our physical condition that we hesitate to take responsibility for our actions.

As I have already indicated, many doctors want to blame our glands, body chemistry, and a host of other causes for depression, but others direct our attention to thought processes or mental attitudes—not our glands. Admittedly, some bodily ailments will affect our mood changes, but even these can be controlled by proper mental attitude. The following diagram will illustrate the point.

The normal mental attitude of a person who walks in the Spirit *most* of the time

Depression produced here when a crisis of life hits at a low time spiritually

The normal circumstances of life = erratic

The above diagram clarifies the importance of maintaining good mental attitudes at all times. We cannot control the circumstances of life, but by the power of the Holy Spirit we can govern our mental attitude. In this diagram the individual indulged in a poor mental attitude three times because of spiritual neglect, sickness, a monthly period or mood cycle, hormone change, sin, or other reasons. During the first two mental-attitude sin periods nothing happened to trigger self-pity, but notice the third. On that occasion, one of those unpredictable circumstances for which life is famous collided with the improper thinking pattern. The predictable result was depression.

When a Christian walks in the Spirit, he will maintain the proper mental attitude so that he can respond in praise and thanksgiving to the negative circumstances of life. Remember, God has promised not to permit negative circumstances above our ability to cope with them. He is, of course, presupposing that we maintain the proper mental attitude.

## What Is the Right Mental Attitude?

Several components make up the right mental attitude. Consider them carefully to see if you possess them.

1) Complete commitment to the will and way of God (Rom. 6:11-13; 12-1, 2).
2) Knowledge of the principles of God (Rom. 12:2). No one will ever know all of the principles of God for living, but you can daily refresh your mind with them by reading and studying the Word of God.
3) Faith (Roman. 14:23 and Heb. 11:6). It is impossible to enlist the dynamic dimensions of God into your life without faith. If your faith is weak, don't wait for some miracle to make it strong. The following steps will strengthen your faith.
   a. Hear, read, and study the Bible (Rom. 13:10).
   b. Pray for increased faith (1 Cor. 12:31).
   c. Walk in the Spirit (Gal. 5:22, 23).
   d. Experience faith (Rom. 1:17). Each time you trust God for something, it is easier to trust Him the next time.

# 13

# Depression and the Occult

My wife is not predisposed to depression by nature, but maintains a very radiant and vibrant personality. One night furnished a distinct exception! On arriving home from work, I found her lethargic, rather somber, and somewhat depressed. The evening meal was not started, nothing seemed to interest her, and I noticed that she sighed heavily. After watching her for a few minutes, I commented, "You're not yourself tonight, dear. What's the matter?" She looked at me and replied, "I don't know. For some reason I just feel depressed." "What have you been doing this afternoon?" "Since bringing the children home at 3:30," she answered, "I've been reading, and gradually this feeling of depression came over me." She handed me a copy of one of the current best sellers regarding the occult, Satanism, and demon possession.

At that point I realized that this book on depression should contain a brief chapter on the emotional effects of reading about the occult. The book she had been pursuing was written by a Christian in a sincere attempt to help other people avoid involvement with the occult. Browsing through the book, I noted that the author gave his own personal experience and many of the intimate details concerning the occult movement and Satan's kingdom of darkness. Frankly, Christians need to know very little about Satan and the occult other than that it is sinful, detrimental, harmful —and something to keep at arm's length.

## The Occult Fad

Ever since his first rebellion against God, Satan has repeatedly attempted to destroy mankind. Primitive cultures have always inclined toward black magic, witchcraft, and other forms of the occult, but invariably to the detriment of the people. Stories by missionaries tell in gruesome detail how association with demon spirits or sophisticated methods of communication with demons produces depression and other forms of human misery. Questions asked in my Family Life Seminars in various parts of the country frequently relate to demonism and the occult. I have seen enough to convince me that all depression is not the result of demon possession or oppression, but all contact with demons or evil spirits produces depression. An individual may consult mystics, Ouija boards, knocking tables, tea-leaf readers, or palmists in any major city, but almost invariably within a few hours or possibly days he will be engulfed by a spirit of depression.

A harmful side effect in today's occult fad finds people tending to blame exorcism or demonism for their behavior. An angry individual would much rather take the irresponsible course by saying, "The devil made me do it!" than admit he is a hostile person.

At times depression leads people to dabble in demonism. Their self-induced misery through protracted periods of self-pity causes them to grope for an easy release of spirit rather than an honest confrontation with the thinking pattern which has brought them down to this slough of despondency. Some resort to drugs or liquor, but mediums, mystics, and necromancers are also readily available as quick solutions. We are familiar with seriously depressed persons, grieving over the loss of a loved one, who have resorted to mediums once again to hear the voice of the departed. But invariably the latter end is worse than the first.

Such panaceas may give short-term relief, but they compound the problem of depression.

A *Campus Life* magazine article quoted Roberta Blankenship, an eighteen-year-old college freshman, who described her experiences as a witch. When asked what common denominator she noticed in those who took up witchcraft, she replied, "First, they all share a deep dissatisfaction with life the way it is—many of these are rather emotional people and there's always something important missing at home."[1] Referring to her own state while being a witch, she admitted, "My depression was almost unbearable."[2] Evidently her periods of depression increased until even witchcraft gave her no satisfaction. "My messed-up world wasn't changing. My home was still full of hate; I had no close friends. In fact, I attempted suicide."[3]

If the truth were known, many modern suicides could probably be attributed to satanically induced depression. An individual who is prone to depression mistakenly thinks witchcraft or the occult offers relief—only to find that his depression is amplified. Then in complete frustration he sees no hope and erroneously concludes that suicide is the only way out. Hal Lindsey in his best selling book, *Satan Is Alive and Well on Planet Earth,* states, ". . . after Satan had used Judas for his purpose, he then used the power of guilt to drive Judas to self-destruction (Matt. 27:5-10). The demon-possessed boy in Matthew 17:14, 15 had a strong tendency toward self-destruction. He threw himself into fire and then into water. This was the result of the demon attempting to inflict harm or self-destruction upon the child."[4]

---

[1]"The Campus Life Forum: Does This Girl Look Like a Witch?" *Campus Life,* p. 16. Reprinted by permission from *Campus Life* Magazine, copyright 1973, Youth for Christ International, Wheaton, Illinois.

[2]*Ibid.,* p. 14.

[3]*Ibid.,* p. 13.

[4]Hal Lindsey, *Satan Is Alive and Well on Planet Earth* (Grand Rapids: Zondervan, 1972), p. 157.

## Deliverance From Demon-Inspired Depression

We can be assured of deliverance from Satan! But that deliverance always occurs on God's terms, not man's or Satan's. If you have entertained the occult, demonism, or any other form of satanic communication or worship, you need to break all relationship with it immediately and turn to Christ. If you are not a Christian, receive Him as your Lord and Savior and then ask to be filled with the Holy Spirit. In the article about Roberta Blankenship quoted above, she excitedly relates her thrilling release from Satan's power. "I found Jesus Christ. He led me out of my darkness. The Bible, much to my surprise, had the *authoritative* answers to my problems. I invited Christ into my life personally, and things really began to change. My hatred vanished, and an unexplainable love began to grow for the people I had hated. *Because I stopped pitying myself, I was ready to reach out and help people.* I found in Christ a Friend I could totally trust . . . Someone who really cared about me with no selfish motives. I reached the end of my loneliness and unhappiness and reached out to Him. And I discovered that Jesus is still the great Healer . . . not physically, in my case, but emotionally. He healed my wracked-up emotions."[5] The deliverance Jesus Christ imparted to young Roberta, He wants to give to you. The joy that results from the Spirit-filled life is the only lasting solution (Eph. 5:18-21).

Once having received Jesus Christ as your personal Lord and Savior, you need only be filled with His Holy Spirit daily and walk in His Spirit (Gal. 5:16-24) to rid yourself of the evil effects of occultism. Remember, God never makes His commandments (Eph. 5:18) impossible or difficult. Since He enjoins us to be filled with the Holy Spirit, it naturally follows that He has made it simple. If you have examined your heart, confessed all known sin, and are totally and un-

---

[5]"The Campus Life Forum: Does This Girl Look Like a Witch?" p. 18.

conditionally yielded to God, then ask to be filled with the Spirit and expect a consistent change in your emotions. The best way to speed the therapy is to read long passages from the Word of God. In fact, begin by a repetitious reading of the Book of Philippians. I have counseled hundreds of depressed-prone people to read the entire Book of Philippians every morning for thirty to sixty days. The truths in that little book will change your outlook on life!

## The Perfect Obsession

During the twenty-six years I have been teaching the Bible I have been requested many times to teach on Satan, demons, and the occult, and some of my friends have suggested that I did not address myself to such subjects often enough. As a rule, I have consistently refused to do so because I find it very harmful for Christians to spend much time thinking about Satan. All of the mystically minded people I know who talk repeatedly about satanism and demons are sad, morbid people. If they understood the function of the human mind, they would realize why. As we have already noted, whatever you project on the imagination screen of your mind will influence your emotions. If you think repeatedly about Satan's devices and ways, you will naturally become depressed. However, if you consciously project the image of the Lord Jesus Christ and the blessings He has brought into your life, your spirit will be lifted. As a reminder of this the Bible charges, "Let this mind be in you, which was also in Christ Jesus," "Looking unto Jesus, the author and finisher of our faith. . . ." When we look to Jesus, He lifts our emotions. Therefore I suggest that you develop the mental hygiene of projecting thoughts about Him on the screen of your mind and avoid thinking about Satan. Anything that continually occupies your mind becomes an obsession and will exercise undue control over you. Never blunder into the pitfall of studying and thinking continually about Satan. A Christian should be obsessed only with Jesus Christ and being continually filled with the Holy Spirit.

Rather than becoming disturbed and even demoralized with the idea that "Satan is going to get me," the Christian can develop emotional and mental maturity through preoccupation with the concept, "My God shall supply all my need." After all, He has promised, "He that is in you is greater than he that is in the world." Let your obsession be with Jesus Christ; then you will defeat Satan every time.

## The Christian's Armor

We are taught in the Word of God, "Resist the devil, and he will flee from you" (James 4:7). Our means of resistance is clearly outlined in Ephesians 6, where we are introduced to the whole armor of God. Note especially that the pieces of armor provide adequate defense for everything but retreat: "Wherefore take unto you the whole armour of God, that ye may be able to withstand in the evil day, and having done all, to stand. Stand therefore, having your loins girt about with truth, and having on the breastplate of righteousness; and your feet shod with the preparation of the gospel of peace; above all, taking the shield of faith, wherewith ye shall be able to quench all the fiery darts of the wicked. And take the helmet of salvation, and the sword of the Spirit, which is the word of God: praying always with all prayer and supplication in the Spirit, and watching thereunto with all perseverance and supplication for all saints" (Eph. 6:13-18).

All the pieces of the Christian's armor in his spiritual warfare are conferred upon him through the Word of God. For this reason it is as essential to read God's Word daily for spiritual nutrition as it is to take in a daily supply of physical food. Anemic Christians whose minds steadily consume the carnal food of television, movies, pornography, and materialism are no match for the devil. They can worry about him, study his methods, become conversant with his program—and still be defeated by him.

By contrast, the Christian who lets the "mind of Christ" become his armor by daily Bible reading and obedience to its teachings will valiantly triumph over

Satan—through the victory that comes only from Christ Jesus. Whenever a Christian sins or is pierced by Satan's dart, he must not concede to his adversary but recognize that defeat is imminent if he fails to appropriate the spiritual armor of the Word of God.

If you are prone to depression or if you find that reading material on the occult has a depressing influence upon you, let me offer this suggestion. The next time you are tempted to read an article or a book concerning Satan or the occult, squelch the desire and read Philippians, Ephesians, 1 John, and the Sermon on the Mount. Your spirit will be uplifted and your emotional life strengthened.

# 14

# Depression and Music

Music has a far greater effect on human emotions than most people realize, for it can invigorate, lift the spirits, depress, and in some cases aggravate. Not only can it create moods, but it can also perpetuate or dispel them.

To discern the power of music over people, watch them during a parade. Their mood changes with the various tunes played by each of the marching bands. In fact, the body tends to sway or pulsate rhythmically in direct proportion to the music, whether folksy or patriotic, lilting or frenzied.

Until modern methods of communication made it possible to be exposed to every kind of music in the world, each culture seemed to gravitate to its own kind of music. To a large extent, the highest musical forms were found in the western civilizations. In fact, the art of music was not really developed to any high degree of proficiency in other countries because of the influence of the various religions on their respective cultures.

Happy music was limited almost exclusively to western civilizations, primarily because until recent years Christianity and Judaism have exercised the largest single influence on western music. Paganism, the chief influence on music in other parts of the world, has always been dominated by the dirge or the chant. Such music heavily utilizes the minor or mournful keys.

In the Old Testament, when man experienced an exhilarating relationship with God, he broke forth into singing. The New Testament similarly indicates that the first characteristic or evidence of the Holy Spirit in the life of a Christian is a song in the heart and praise through melody (Eph. 5:18-20). As a result, Christianity has contributed to the world some of its greatest music and musical forms, designed by God as an instrument of blessing to man's emotions.

In a previous chapter we demonstrated that man's emotions are influenced by his mind. Music furnishes an exception to that rule, for like medication or drugs, it is able to influence the emotions while bypassing the mind. For that reason, just as you regulate the kind of medication or drugs your family uses, it is important that you govern the kind of music you and your family hear.

## Music Affects Your Moods

In this age of depression, modern music often tends to be depressing, either because the people who write the music are depressed and the music reflects their mood, or because the music itself is depressing. Quite often both are true. Some blame Satan for this detrimental use of music in an attempt to demoralize people. I am inclined to consider it as the natural result of eliminating Jesus Christ from one's life.

If you examine carefully the words of many popular tunes, you will find them unusually filled with complaint and lamentation. Gloom and disaster seem to constitute the foreboding element in modern music. The last thing a depressed person needs is to hear this kind of music! But strangely enough, because of his depressed mood he may indeed gravitate to that music.

The once happy music of the West, because of the atheistic control of the communications media, is rapidly degenerating into the same depressing tunes I heard in India, Africa, and China. Unless a musician is filled with the Holy Spirit, he will tend to create morbid, pessimistic, negative music that features a detrimental beat or tune. We need a return to happy music today.

As I drove away from Forest Lawn Cemetery in Los Angeles one day, I was amazed to find myself singing. It had just been my privilege to participate in the funeral service for a very dear friend and teacher who had been a significant spiritual blessing in my life. My first reaction to the spontaneous song I felt was one of guilt, because traditionally we are supposed to be sad after leaving the funeral of a loved one. Upon reflection, I found that my mood echoed the "Hallelujah Chorus" sung at the close of the service. At his request, that jubilant song declaring the Christian's triumphant victory over death, had supplanted traditional sadness with joy.

The capability of music to affect our moods has been well established. As far back as the days of King Saul of Israel, when taken in a "vexation of spirit" (probably a spirit of depression), he called for David, the sweet psalmist of Israel, to come and play on his harp. The beautiful strains of the harp in the hands of a spiritual instrumentalist had a lifting effect on Saul's mood (1 Sam. 16:23).

## Music in the Home

Every home should be filled with music, but not just any kind of music. Wholesome, inspiring background music has a tendency to reduce minor sources of irritation and unpleasant noises around the home. In addition, it can lift the mood of children and adults. Because Sunday morning seems to foment so much irritation and conflict in Christian homes as the family dashes through breakfast, scurries to finish last-minute chores, and finally heads discordantly for Sunday school, the wise parent, aware of the hectic scramble that Sunday morning occasions, but also conscious of the soothing effect of music, lets the radio or stereo fill the house with strains of praise and exaltation. No one awakening to "A Mighty Fortress Is Our God" or "Jesus Shall Reign" can growl through breakfast!

Someone who has made a thorough study of the influence of music on the home suggests that we ought to play rousing music in the morning, active music in the afternoon, and restful music in the evening. I am convinced that one of the best ways a Christian family can counteract the nearly universal tendency of young people to favor hard rock or mournful ballads, which are usually detrimental to their emotional development, is to provide them with a creative alternative. Only in so doing will we create in them a wholesome appetite for good music.

If you or someone in your family is susceptible to depression, you are advised to select your music carefully. Make sure that whatever the music or instrument, it has a joyous, lifting effect upon your emotions. Don't let your circumstances determine the music, and reject music that matches your mood. Instead provide yourself with music that will exercise a positive influence on you and your household.

It would be hard to find a more difficult place for singing than a prison cell. Yet the Apostle Paul, together with Silas his traveling companion, used such an occasion to elevate their spirits by singing. Acts 16 relates their imprisonment for preaching the Gospel and casting out an evil spirit from a young girl. They were not only confined to a jail cell but severely beaten and left with their hands and feet in stocks. Instead of complaining to God and feeling sorry for themselves, they began to sing and praise Him. As a result they were in a spiritual frame of mind to be instruments of God in leading the first Europeans to a saving knowledge of Jesus Christ, which maintained and even further elevated their high spirits.

The Bible teaches that a heart free of guilt and at one with God produces a spontaneous and joyous hymn of thanksgiving. A life and heart void of God has a tendency to produce and respond to dissident, sorrowful music. The writer of Proverbs 29:6 explains that "the righteous doth sing and rejoice," and throughout the Bible we find that a person's relationship to God and knowledge of His wonderful ways and works produces singing. Consider the following: "Sing unto the LORD; for he hath done excellent things: this is known in all the earth" (Isa. 12:5). "Sing, O ye heavens; for the LORD hath done it: shout, ye lower parts of the earth: break forth into singing, ye mountains, O forest, and every tree therein: for the LORD hath redeemed Jacob, and glorified himself in Israel" (Isa. 44:23).

The great singer of Israel exclaimed, "Make a joyful noise unto the LORD, all ye lands. Serve the LORD with gladness: come before his presence with singing. Know ye that the LORD he is God: it is he that hath made us, and not we ourselves; we are his people, and the sheep of his pasture. Enter into his gates with thanksgiving, and into his courts with praise: be thankful unto him, and bless his name. For the LORD is good; his mercy is everlasting; and his truth endureth to all generations" (Ps. 100).

The emotional aftermath of joyous, lifting music is highly beneficial, similar to the results of thanksgiving thinking and conversation. The proper kind of music will greatly assist your feelings of well-being and help you avoid the tendency to depression. Just as depression feeds depression, so joy feeds joy. Music can help create the right kind of mental attitude that when followed by the right kind of thought patterns will help you avoid depression.

# 15

# Ten Steps to Victory Over
# Depression

No one enjoys depression, though everyone has fallen victim to it during his lifetime. Some experience it more than others, depending on how much self-pity he has indulged in. By this time we have established the fact that it's not a consequence of "body chemistry," "other people," or "the pressures of life," but our own mental attitude toward those pressures which induce depression.

It has been my purpose in this book to show that depression is unnecessary and can be avoided! This chapter contains the ten steps you can take to escape the problem. Hundreds of people having tried these steps and have testified to their reliability.

A twenty-four-year-old woman who came in for counseling acknowledged many years of depression. During the preceding four years she had undergone thirty electric-shock treatments for the malady—and was nothing bettered. In fact, her problem was compounded by a loss of memory. She had lost at least two years of her life in sanitariums due to depression.

Looking into the face of this attractive young woman, I couldn't help thinking how her case was so typical of the severely depressed. To begin with, she was predominantly melancholy in temperament: consequently she was negative, sensitive, and overly oc-

cupied with herself. In addition, she had lost all hope
for the future. The product of a broken home, she was
literally unwanted by either parent or her brothers and
sisters.

The first step in Beth's remarkable recovery was
taken when she accepted Jesus Christ as her personal
Lord and Savior. He provided the assurance of love
and forgiveness she had always longed for. He also
provided her with the power to overcome her thought
patterns of resentment and self-pity. By gaining the
ability from Him to forgive her parents, she removed
the root of bitterness that had immobilized her for years.

Three months after her conversion she discon-
tinued the drugs prescribed by her psychiatrist and experienced the best emotional stability of her life. She
revisited her psychiatrist at our suggestion, because
she felt guilty at not formally terminating her treatments. He was overjoyed at the change in his patient
and immediately jumped to the conclusion that his
combination of drug therapy and psychotherapy had
finally brought her relief. When she informed him that
she had became a Christian and that Christ had brought
a whole new way of life to her, it must have been a
threat to him, for he immediately lashed out at her in
a most unprofessional manner. He warned her that
"it will not last! Christianity is only a crutch; you will
be back here in a few weeks worse off than you were
before." She informed him that she was no longer
taking his drugs and was sleeping better than ever. He
berated both her faith and her intelligence.

Fortunately, Beth drove straight to my office. All
she needed was some biblical reassurance to the reality
of her experience. We once again reviewed the steps
to overcoming depression that had already helped her.
Gradually her confidence and joy returned, and she
left my office to continue living that abundant Christian
life the Lord has promised to all His children who
meet His conditions. If her experience with Christ is
only a "crutch," it must be a pretty good one, because
it has been almost a year now since she has been
depressed, in spite of the fact that her family circum-

stances and living conditions have actually gotten worse.

Your depression, or that of someone you love, that has caused you to read this book is probably not nearly as severe as was Beth's. But these steps to victory over depression that have proven so effective for her will prove equally beneficial to you if you use them.

(1) *Accept Jesus Christ as your Savior*—With all due respect to the powers of your mind and will, you do not have the capacity to avoid depression without help from God. One of the tragic blunders of modern psychology, success motivation, or other humanistic forms of self-improvement lies in its presumption that man does not need God's help to lift him out of depression. Jesus Christ said, ". . . without me ye can do nothing" (John 15:5), and this is particularly true of depression. If you anticipate victory over depression on a lasting basis, you must begin by inviting Jesus Christ into your life. Once you have done that, as we described the experience in chapter 6, you will then possess the divine resources of God to enable you to take the next nine steps for victory over depression. If you are not sure you have had such an experience, I would counsel you first of all to slip to your knees and personally invite Him into your life. Be assured of the promise, "For whosoever shall call upon the name of the Lord shall be saved" (Rom. 10:13).

(2) *Walk in the Spirit*—Accepting Jesus Christ as your personal Savior and walking in the Spirit on a day-to-day basis are not identical experiences. The latter, of course, is made possible by the first. The steps for being filled by the Spirit, considered in chapter 9, should be followed carefully.

The most important step in being filled with the Spirit is the total commitment of your life to Christ. The self-life always causes depression. Making Christ Lord of your life each day enables you to avoid self-pity, self-indulgence, self-centeredness, and the many natural expressions of selfishness.

## Who Controls Your Life?

It is not difficult to determine whether or not your life is committed to Christ at any given time. Just ask yourself, "Who is in control of my life right now?" The throne below symbolizes the free will of man. Only one person can sit as Lord on the throne of your life at one time, you or Jesus Christ. The "S" on the throne of a carnal Christian represents his self. Christ is in his life but is not allowed to control it. Such living, which unfortunately is all too common, constitutes a miserable state of existence. Christians who remain at the helm of their lives become unproductive and unattractive. Nothing about their lives exemplifies the change that Christ brings, for their self-directed program and ego-centered perspective belie their position as new creatures in Christ Jesus. Some would even dare to ask God's blessing upon their selfish designs, but this doesn't exempt them from misery and emptiness.

The Christ-controlled life steadily wins over depression. Jesus Christ, by His Holy Spirit, sits on the throne of this person's life, directing his thoughts, feelings, and actions.

Life embraces an endless number of decisions, large and small. Where shall I live? What shall I pursue as a life vocation? Whom shall I marry? Either you or Jesus Christ will make these decisions. The life of faith and commitment to Christ places all decisions in His hands. The Bible teaches, "In all thy ways acknowledge him, and he shall direct thy paths" (Prov. 3:6).

The illustration on page 191 describes that decision-making process with the following diagram and dots, each dot representing a decision in life.

The carnal Christian runs his own life and makes his own decisions, whereas the Christ-controlled Christian turns them over to Jesus Christ by prayerfully asking, "Lord Jesus, how do You want me to handle this situation?" "Do You want me to take this job opportunity?" "How do You want me to respond to

CARNAL CHRISTIAN

my wife, or husband, or children, or boss, or neighbors?"

The practical differences in the two life styles are clearly listed in the above diagram. The self-controlled life is miserable. The Christ-controlled life is dynamic! One propagates disarray and confusion, inducing self to stagger from crisis to crisis. The Christ-controlled life guarantees peace and confidence, thus avoiding many crises (because it is supernaturally directed), and with confidence faces those inescapable crises as they come. This believer is confident that his Director will abundantly supply every need.

I had just come in from water skiing on San Diego Bay with my sons when we met a college student named Bill. He began to tell me what Christ meant to him personally and how He was controlling his entire life. Since I hadn't seen him in church for several weeks, I asked which church he was attending regularly. (I have found that Christians cannot walk in the Spirit very long unless they go *regularly* to a Bible-teaching church where they can feed their mind, heart, and spirit on the Word of God.) He replied, "Oh, I haven't been going anywhere lately." "What do you do on Sunday mornings, Bill?" He honestly replied, "I sleep in." "But I thought you were letting Jesus Christ control your life now." Rather peevishly he retorted,

"I don't have to go to church to be a good Christian." "No," I said, "but if Jesus Christ is in control of your life at 9:30 on Sunday morning, what do you think He would have you do?" Then his subtle self-indulgent thought processes came to the fore. "Sunday is the only day I have to sleep in. I work and study hard all week long, and I think I deserve one day to relax and do my thing." When I confronted him with the fact that his excuse contained five personal pronouns and totally excluded Jesus Christ, he suddenly realized that he had never consulted Christ about his Sunday morning decision.

I had the advantage in that conversation because I already knew what Jesus Christ's decision would be. Hebrews 10:25 says, "Not forsaking the assembling of ourselves together, as the manner of some is; but exhorting one another: and so much the more, as ye see the day approaching."

When confronted with any decision in life, prayerfully ask, "Lord Jesus, what about this?" Usually a verse of Scripture or a biblical principle will pop into your mind and cast light on the subject. If you act in that light, you will make a proper decision; if you don't, you will once again be thrown into the den of error. Never ask, "What do I want to do about this?" True spiritual maturity, the product of time spent in the Word and continuous walking in the Spirit, manifests itself when Christ's will and your will are synonymous.

Depression-prone people should scrutinize their thought processes to see if they are controlled by Jesus Christ. His control does not tolerate self-pitying thoughts, and consequently Christ-controlled living is depression-free living.

## The Results of the Spirit-Filled Life

Though everyone wants the results of the Spirit-filled life, few people experience them. I have never met anyone who premeditatedly set out to make himself miserable, but most people do! By running their own lives selfishly, they create inordinate distress.

In this regard, Ephesians 5:18-21 becomes a crucial passage for Christians. It should be memorized and contemplated daily. After commanding us to be continually filled (or controlled) by the Holy Spirit, it specifies the results. Note them carefully:

Verse 19—a song in your heart

Verse 20—a thanksgiving attitude

Verse 21—a submissive spirit

You will never find a miserable person with a song in his heart, a thanksgiving attitude, and a submissive spirit! Nor will you find a happy person without them. And isn't happiness what *everyone* wants out of life? Unfortunately, people try to achieve their happiness through the mental, emotional, or physical areas of life, but it cannot be found there. Only by turning one's life and all of its decisions over to Christ can one ever gain lasting happiness!

(3) *Forgive those who sin against you!*—It is impossible to walk in the Spirit for a protracted period of time while refusing to obey Christ's command to "forgive those who trespass against you" (Matt. 6:12). Depressed-prone individuals are always conscious of a loved one or relative who rejected or injured them earlier in life. Until they forgive that person, they will never know lasting victory over depression. In fact, they will never develop spiritual maturity either. Jesus said, "For if ye forgive men their trespasses, your heavenly Father will also forgive you: *But if ye forgive not men their trespasses, neither will your Father forgive your trespasses*" (Matt. 6:14, 15).

The unforgiving spirit of a carnal Christian is harmful spiritually, mentally, emotionally, and physically. You have doubtless heard the expression, "He burns me up!" Little does a person realize that the bitterness festering in his mind will destroy his relationship with God and man.

An unforgiving attitude is never limited to one person. Like cancer in the body, it is a mental disease that feeds on itself until it severs the expression of love and other wholesome emotions. In addition, it makes an invalid of its subject, a prey to every gust of passion. Bitterness tends to expand and intensify through the years until even little things arouse his rancorous spirit. I have found that a bitter, unforgiving thought pattern toward someone you hate will even minimize or limit your expressions of love for someone you love.

If you would sincerely rid yourself of depression, ask yourself, "Is there anyone in life I have never forgiven?" If so, confess that sin to God immediately and ask God to take away that habit pattern. If the individual is aware of your resentment or bitterness, apologize personally if possible or by mail. Admittedly, this is a very difficult gesture, but it is essential for emotional stability.

A Christian couple came in for marriage counseling with several surface problems but no deep-rooted difficulties that I could find. In talking to the man, who seemed to be the primary source of friction in the home, I found that years before he had suffered a tragic experience with a business partner and had steadfastly harbored this affront and indulged in bitterness throughout the years. His resentful thinking pattern was not only a sin, but was also a mental habit pattern that spoiled his relationship with other people, including his wife. This bitterness was probably a major reason why the man had never become a mature and effective Christian. Finally recognizing his problem, he made an appointment with the man and asked his forgiveness. To his amazement, he found that eighteen months previously this man had become a Christian and had likewise been convicted about the matter. Today they are reasonably good friends, and a major source of irritation in the marriage of this couple has been removed. The elimination of that root of bitterness has improved his entire thinking pattern and strengthened his spiritual and emotional life to such a degree that business associates notice the change in him.

All causes of bitterness need not be real, but in some cases exist only in the imagination. One deeply depressed young woman came to me after an unhappy courtship explosion. As the author of the breakup, she concluded that she lacked a normal attitude toward the opposite sex. Sensing that it was abnormal to be so cold and indifferent to marriage, she came in for help. I understood enough about her background to know that she was raised by a divorced mother who sacrificed everything for her daughter during he childhood. When the girl was twelve her mother remarried a fine Christian man who adopted her as his own child and tried his best to raise her properly as a daughter.

This nineteen-year-old girl was consumed with a spirit of bitterness toward her loving and devoted mother because she "smothered and dominated my every decision." Unfortunately, the mother, blaming herself for the breakup of her first marriage, had bent over backwards to make it up to the daughter and consequently had become overprotective. (A parent raising children alone must realize that God is able to supply the needs of a child raised with only one parent in the home.) Some bright-eyed college sophomore with a psychology book under his arm informed her that she was overly dependent upon her mother. As a result she built up an artificial case of resentment until it spilled over and stifled her normal emotions toward others. Only by confessing her sins of resentment and ingratitude to God and by writing a letter of apology to her mother was she able to be restored spiritually, emotionally and mentally.

Someone has sagely remarked, "Forgive or perish." The human mind is so constructed that if you protract bitterness and hatred toward someone, it will ultimately destroy you.

(4) *Renew your mind daily*—As we have already seen, the way to consistently transform your life is to renew your mind with the Word of God. The way of this world is so contrary to the ways of God that it is nearly impossible to find any spiritual help in the secular world. Therefore, just as you nourish your body on a daily basis, you should feed your mind those things that will contribute to your spiritual development. All such wisdom comes from God and is found in His library of divine truth called the Holy Bible. Only by reading, studying, meditating, memorizing, and hearing His wisdom will you become the mature Christian

that God wants you to be, established in the faith and competent to overcome tendencies toward depression.

(5) *Practice creative imagery daily through prayer* —In chapter 11 we examined the importance of fashioning a wholesome image of yourself and your goals on the screen of your imagination daily. By way of review, the following suggests a brief step-by-step method. (These are the ten steps to victory over depression.)

    a. *Accept yourself as a creature of God.*
       Thank God that you are an object of His love and that He made you as you are. Make a special point of thanking Him for whatever part of your nature or looks you are apt to regret. Since it is impossible to change, and since God controls the genes at conception, it is an act of disobedience to resent those areas of your life that cannot be changed. Thank Him for what you are and trust Him to gradually make you the person He wants you to be.

    b. *Accept God's forgiveness for your sins.*
       If you find sin in your life, of course, confess it. But whenever you examine yourself on the screen of your imagination, you will quite naturally focus upon the mistakes and sins of the past. Once having confessed them, be sure to thank God for His forgiveness. Accepting God's forgiveness would mean that you see yourself as clothed in the righteousness of Jesus, not in the raggedness of your sins. "He that overcometh, the same shall be clothed in white raiment; and I will not blot out his name out of the book of life, but I will confess his name before my Father, and before his angels" (Rev. 3:5).

    c. *Superimpose God onto your self-image.*
       Thank God for His presence in your life in a real and practical way, reminding your-

self as did the apostle Paul, "I *can* do all things *through Christ* which strengtheneth me" (Phil. 4:13).

d. *Visualize yourself as God is shaping you.* Resist the temptation to see yourself in the light of failures past, but envision yourself as growing and maturing as both you and God desire you to be. One mother confined to a small home with three preschool children found this practice helpful in learning to control her temper. For some time she had viewed herself on the screen of her imagination as an ill-tempered, irrational mother gradually losing control of herself because of the heavy demands of her children. The more she saw herself in such a light, the more she acted this way. By visualizing herself daily as Christ would have her become, she gradually learned to respond more patiently and graciously in obedience to the Spirit's control of her life. Naturally, the more patience she actuated, the more she reinforced the positive image on the screen of her imagination. This in turn made it easier for her to be controlled and patient. The Bible tells us, "Let this mind be in you which is also in Christ Jesus." Think of yourself as a reflection of the mind of Christ. How would He treat children under those circumstances? Or how would He respond to an irate boss or a demanding, domineering parent? See yourself reacting as Christ would and you will find yourself gradually sustaining that reaction.

e. *Visualize by faith your basic life goals and write them down.*

By noting your objectives and writing them down, you activate your subconscious mind to remind you of those things needing to be done in order to fulfill your goals.

By praying about them in faith, you also summon the power of God on your behalf, which makes it possible to achieve the impossible.

*f. Always be positive.*

There is no place in the Christian's life for negativism. Linked as we are with the divine power of God, we should never anticipate anything but success. Avoid the complainer, the griper, and the critic; most of all, avoid imitating them. The personnel director of a large corporation who had learned the powerful influence of negativism on people explained to me why he selected one particular man over another for a special job assignment. I knew both men and volunteered my surprise at his selection, for I felt that the man he passed over was the more effective employee. He responded, "I never hire a top echelon executive until I first interview his wife. Although I am aware of the tremendous capabilities of our mutual friend, I am also conscious of the excessive griping habits to which his wife is given. I therefore conclude that she would have a harmful, demotivating influence on his work. I chose the other man because I judged that the margin between them would easily be bridged by the supportive role of his wife."

Negativism, pessimism, griping, criticism, and gossip are not only harmful but also contagious. In fact, you reinforce them in your own mind every time you verbalize them. Keep your conversation *and* your mind positive at all times. Listen to the most powerful instruction on this subject in Scripture: "Finally, brethren, whatsoever things are true, whatsoever things are honest, whatsoever things are just, whatsoever things are pure, whatsoever things are lovely, whatsoever things are of good report; if there be any virtue, and if there be any praise, think on these things" (Phil. 4:8).

    g. *Anticipate the superabundant life God has in store for you.*

God has fashioned a complete plan for your life, but it is flexible. It includes the good, acceptable, and perfect will of God. Romans 12:1 says, "I beseech you therefore, brethren, by the mercies of God, that ye present your bodies a living sacrifice, holy, acceptable unto God, which is your reasonable service."

| Man's Needs | Man's Desires |
|---|---|
| "My God shall supply all your need" | "That your joy may be full" |

God's Abundance
Exceeding abundantly above
all you can ask or think.
"According to your faith be it unto you"

We read in Philippians 4:19, "But my God shall supply all your need according to his riches in glory by Christ Jesus." Concerning His desire to supply your wholesome, God-honoring wants, John 16:24 promises, "Hitherto have ye asked nothing in my name: ask, and ye shall receive, that your joy may be full." In addition, He desires to shower you "exceeding abundantly above all" that you could ever ask or think (Eph. 3:20).

Most Christians spend their lives on the left-hand portion of the chart, asking God to supply their needs. I never *ask* Him to supply my need because He has already promised to do that. Years ago I found in John 16:24 that God loves to make me happy by supplying those things that I want and providing these wants in accord with His basic plan for my life. In more recent years, I have found that God is a Father who enjoys giving to His children. In fact, Jesus Christ compared an earthly father with the heavenly Father when He said, "If ye then, being evil, know how to give good gifts unto your children, *how much more* shall your Father which is in heaven give good things to them that ask him?" (Matt. 7:11).

One day after a wonderful Christmas at our home, it dawned on me that it is thrilling and satisfying to be a parent. We have always received much pleasure and enjoyment in giving to our children, even in excess of their wants. Most parents are like that. We don't give because they deserve it, because most children today already possess more than they deserve. Rather, we parents give to our children purely because we love them. If that is true of us, how much more is it true of God! He wants to give you "exceeding abundantly above all that we ask or think"! Never limit God by unbelief, but anticipate that He will perform something supernatural in your life. Remember, "According to your faith be it unto you." Your success does not depend on your opportunity or ability, but on your faith. If your faith is weak, ask God to grant you more faith that you in turn may anticipate the power of a supernatural and superabundant God working in your life.

### h. Seek first the kingdom of God.

Matthew 6:33 makes it clear that the Christian can make no allowance for greed or self-motive in his life. Although he may seek employment or material gain, he can never let it become his primary objective. Instead, his first objective should be to seek the kingdom of God and His righteousness. Any time our quest for material gain runs contrary to the kingdom of God or His righteousness, it is wrong for us. Even if we were successful in achieving some degree of prosperity while doing something contrary to the will of God, it would not be a lasting source of enjoyment. Remember, it is essential that you be obedient to God. In establishing your priorities, consider the first commandment, "Thou shalt love the Lord thy God with all thy heart, soul, and mind." You can judge your sincere love for God by whether or

not you serve Him. If your first objective
is to earn a living and to stockpile this
world's goods, then you not only demonstrate your greed, but also a lack of sufficient love for God. Give God His right-
ful place in your heart, express it in your
attitude toward things, and He will bless
you with items you need, provisions "exceeding abundantly above all that you ask
or think."

*i. Give yourself to God to serve people.*
The most rewarding and gratifying experiences in life come in serving people. This
will be emotionally therapeutic. Depressed
people are inclined to spend too much
time thinking about themselves. Serving
God by helping people forces you to think
about someone besides yourself. I am personally convinced that God has oriented
the human psyche in such a way that unless
a man befriends others, he cannot be satisfied with himself. The rewards of such
service are not only beneficial for eternity,
but also helpful in this life.

One seriously depressed woman decided that she
had never really helped anyone since her children
went off to school. Although she had taught Sunday
school in her earlier years, the birth of three small
children directed her energies elsewhere. When she
was free during the day, she considered it essential
to "rest up," but finally she was overcome by depression. As we talked, she realized it was time for her to
recognize that God could use her as a means of reaching her neighbors for Christ, so she started a women's
Bible class on Wednesdays. Several weeks later she
had become a very dynamic, outgoing woman. While
visiting casually at a social activity, I smilingly inquired,
"How is your depression lately?" I shall never forget
her response. She laughed aloud, and with a twinkle in
her eye said, "I don't have time to be depressed anymore!" The fact that several of her neighbors had

found Christ and two families were spared a disastrous breakup in their marriages had given her a new purpose for living and a sense of self-esteem.

The Bible teaches, "Give, and it shall be given unto you; good measure, pressed down, and shaken together, and running over, shall men give into your bosom. For with the same measure that ye mete withal it shall be measured to you again" (Luke 6:38). Scripture also promises, "He that findeth his life shall lose it: and he that loseth his life for my sake shall find it" (Matt. 10:39). If you would really live free from depression, stop hoarding your life and give it away.

### j. In everything give thanks.

"In every thing give thanks: for this is the will of God in Christ Jesus concerning you" (1 Thess. 5:18). That verse offers an absolute guarantee against emotional depression! For several years in family conferences before thousands of people I have announced, "I can give you a money-back guarantee that will keep you from ever being depressed again. It is found in 1 Thessalonians 5:18." So far I have not encountered a single exception. There is just no way a healthy person filled with the Holy Spirit, rendering thanks in everything, can become depressed.

In recent years I have noted a new emphasis upon this matter of giving thanks that has injected lasting joy into the lives of millions of Christians. We may approach thanksgiving in two contrasting ways: consciously by sight or consciously by faith. Consider them individually:

(1) *Give thanks consciously by sight*—The Bible repeatedly advises gratitude as the ideal mental attitude. A grateful person is a happy person. Counting our many blessings to see what God has already done in our lives develops an optimistic faith to trust Him for the future.

Depressed people are usually ungrateful people who in turn become unhappy people. I have found it therapeutic to ask such people to list those things for which they are grateful and review this record once or twice a day, thanking God in prayer for these blessings. The results are absolutely amazing. Some counselees have been so morose and unappreciative that I have actually had to help them work up their list. But once it was made, they began to catch the spirit of praise and discover far more to be grateful for than they had realized. Rehearsing objects of thanksgiving consistently for one week revitalized their mental attitudes and dispelled all sorrow and despondence.

(2) *Consciously give thanks by faith*—At times in life it is impossible to understand God's dealings with us, usually because we lack the divine perspective. God sees not only the present circumstances but also the end result, extending His provision on a long-term, permanent basis. Unfortunately, we are usually more concerned with the immediate and, consequently, when circumstances annoy or displease us, we are prone to gripe mentally rather than "give thanks in everything." For that reason it is essential that we learn to give thanks by faith.

We have already seen that our computer-like mind will reject the impossible. Humanly speaking, giving thanks "in everything" is unreasonable and inconceivable, a violation of logic. For that reason we must learn to program God into the situation and recognize that He has a plan, including even the most unhappy circumstances which work for our long-range good. Therefore, as an expression of our faith and confidence in His love and ability to act in our behalf, we should "in everything give thanks, for this is the will of God in Christ Jesus concerning you."

## Thanksgiving as a Habit

Just as we form bad habits, we also create good habits. Most of us brush our teeth every day, not because we enjoy the process, but because we recognize its value. Consequently we have developed the habit. By the same token we can create the good habit of giving thanks in everything in obedience to the will of God. Refusal to be obedient in this regard can make you depressed at almost a moment's notice, because the unexpected circumstances of life are bound to strike at the most inopportune time. If you react negatively, you will experience emotional depression and become spiritually useless to God at that precise moment.

Lest you think these are idle words and not genuine experience, let me share with you my own predicament as I write this section. In twenty-five years I have never missed a preaching assignment, although I have had some close calls. At 11:50 this morning I completed a pastor's seminar in Amarillo, Texas. Seated on a Continental Airlines 727, I was expecting to arrive in Dallas at 2:20 and catch a 3:00 flight to Atlanta, Georgia, where I was to begin a Family Life Seminar at 7:00 P.M. At 12:55, as we were taxiing out to the runway area, I watched the pilot suddenly turn the plane around and head back to the landing station. A few moments later I saw him deplane, meet with a mechanic, and begin taking the cover off one of the engines. Subsequently a thirty-minute delay was announced. A few minutes later the mechanic brought a piece of cable out of the engine, held it up, and gave the pilot a message. Within a few seconds I heard over the P.A. system that a defective part would have to be replaced and that the flight was cancelled.

Walking inside the air terminal, I practiced what I have just written. "Praise the Lord." God knew that the next flight from Amarillo to Dallas arrived eleven minutes after the Dallas to Atlanta flight. When this information was confirmed, I asked Him for guidance and then called an air charter service at another airport. The pilot assured me that for $200 I could be flown privately to Dallas and arrive on time. Although I thoroughly enjoyed the flight, we landed just as my Delta flight lifted off the runway at Love Field. "Now what am I going to do?" I knew the choice was mine. I could grumble, be miserable, or praise the Lord and just let Him take care of the details. So I decided to take the biblical course, and here I sit, finishing this chapter.

The Director of Family Life Seminars just had me paged over the loudspeaker system. After I informed him that I could not get into Atlanta until 9:30 to-night, fifteen minutes *after* the seminar concluded, he asked, "What am I going to do?" "Why not praise the Lord?" As I write this, I am fully conscious that some rather irate Atlantans may be attending our seminar, but I can expect the heavenly Father to provide for their needs in ways I do not have any manner of fore-seeing. Of one thing I am certain: I have done the will of God to the best of my ability, I have faced uncon-trollable circumstances with joy, and I can therefore sit back without worry or agitation, trusting Him to work out the details. Doubtless He has something in mind in this experience that I know nothing about.

As I walked by the ticket counter and heard the angry passengers berating the ticket agent, I couldn't help but think, "Why can't everyone learn the secret of living by faith, that they too might 'in everything give thanks'?" The day may come when I will under-stand by sight the delay and the suspended engage-ment, but then again, I may not. Of one thing I am certain: shrill lamentations and prayers of protesta-tion, which would reflect my natural temperament ten-dency, will not help a bit. At a time like this a succinct biblical principle encourages me: "My times are in thy hand" (Ps. 31:15). Whatever His reason for wanting me to miss that flight, I can trust Him to know what is best for me.[1]

## Are You a Groaner or a Praiser?

My friend Ken Poure, who has been greatly used of God in family conferences throughout the nation, suggests that our reaction at times like this exhibits our spiritual maturity. He proposes that the time lapse

---

[1]For the curious, that night the F. L. S. Director shared two Family Life films by Dr. Henry Brandt which really met the needs of the people. When I began the following morning, they were in an excellent mood and we enjoyed an exciting seminar. Had I resorted to worry, agitation, or anxiety while waiting in Dallas, it would obviously have been an exercise in futility. God knows what He is doing!

between one's knowledge of a disappointing experience and his praising the Lord by faith will reveal the strength of his spiritual life. If you can rejoice in a matter of moments, you are spiritual. If it takes you fifteen minutes to an hour, you are still growing. If an hour or several days pass, "you are in real trouble," Ken warns. Then he asks a very perceptive question: "Are you a praiser or a groaner?" Most people are one or the other. The sooner you learn to praise God in the face of adverse circumstances or frustrated expectations, the happier you will be and the more you will live a depression-free life.

# 16

# How to Help Your Children Avoid Depression

To our dismay as parents, the tendency to depression sometimes begins at a very early age. The depressed child will usually withdraw and become abnormally quiet and seclusive. He will sulk or hide from group activities at play, hoping someone will notice his pain. Because parents are often the last to recognize depression in their children, their frustration and anger at the child's withdrawal may compound the difficulty before they become fully aware of it.

If the depressed child does not withdraw, he tends to nurse his resentments until they erupt in such erratic behavior that he earns the reputation of being "a problem child." He may break things to get attention, fight with other children, and in general make himself "Peck's bad boy." Such behavior should be interpreted by his parents as a cry for help. He craves love, affection, and reassurance from them, but instead their exasperation at his behavior only amplifies his feeling of rejection. This lowers his self-esteem, increases his anger, and produces further obnoxious behavior.

Statistics indicate that suicide may well accompany such a condition. Because children often live in a fantasy world and through television feed upon violence, they have no comprehension of the finality of death. Therefore, determined to get even with their parents by some act of self-destruction, while at the same time hoping to return to life (as some individuals do on television), depressed children resort to suicide. This is becoming an alarming tragedy of our times. And even if the depressed child escapes self-destruction, he is almost certain to develop the dreadful habit of self-rejection. A negative thinking pattern or failure complex can well leave him emotionally and mentally scarred for life.

The adopted son of a couple caused such concern because of his erratic behavior that his parents came for counseling. Although the boy had developed a reputation in school for being "stupid," "inept," and "bungling," in reality he had an I.Q. in excess of 145 and knew as much about science and electronics as many engineers. By drawing deeply upon spiritual resources and administering unusual love, acceptance, and approval, the parents brought that boy out of his tendency to depression.

For every home which has been blessed with children, the following sixteen suggestions may serve as a checklist of children's special needs:

(1) *Love and affection*—The primary cause of depression in children, lack of love and affection from their parents, sets up thought patterns of resentment and self-pity. God has so constructed the mental mechanism of a child that he automatically looks to his parents for affection. A child's emotional need for love matches his physical need for food.

In my opinion, one reason so many adults encounter recurring depression today is that they were not breast-fed as babies. Humanistic man in his determination to effect a way of life independent of God made the mistake of suggesting to young mothers that modern science had produced a substitute for mother's milk. But he failed to take into account that a bottle in a crib is no substitute for a mother's love.

A group of Jewish doctors set up a special clinic in New York for Jewish orphans. They spared no hygienic means to protect the babies from germs, even to using special germ-killing lights, filtering the air, and requiring that attendants put on new sterile uniforms and rubber gloves when feeding the little ones. Much to their horror, they discovered that the mortality rate in their hospital was three times higher than in a similar hospital in Mexico. An investigator was dispatched to find what the Mexican hospital contained which theirs did not. When the report came back, they could hardly believe it! The understaffed Mexican hospital, lacking in registered nurses, unsanitary by New York standards, and totally inadequate according to the rules of modern medicine, adhered faithfully to a rather "odd rule." Every baby was held in the arms of an attendant at feeding time.

As important as the mother's milk is to the child physically, so is the tenderness and reassurance of a mother's love to the child's emotions. I am deeply convinced that the Creator had this vital relationship in mind when He designed both the mother's body and the child's emotions.

All children crave affection, even the most choleric child. If he receives it at this stage, he tends to develop into normality and finds it easy to express affection. The love-starved child will either become cold or develop an obsessive compulsion for affection. When our first child was a preschooler, we boarded children. I will never forget the olive-skinned four-year-old named Carol who lived in our home for one year. She had been abandoned by her mother, no one knew the identity of her father, and she had lived in eight different homes by the time she came to us. I never saw a child who craved so much kissing. Whenever I showered kisses on our Linda, Carol would demand many more—and always insisted that I kiss her squarely on the mouth. Sometimes it took the supernatural love of God to bestow sufficient love upon that child, but I can testify that He supplies that need.

(2) *Acceptance*—The need for acceptance by those closest to us in life is well-known. In fact, many children are afraid they really do not belong to their parents or seem apprehensive lest a mistake was made in bringing them home from the hospital. Not only their relationship with parents in the home, but also

their appearance, capabilities, and habits are in need
of acceptance. The child who is conscious that he is
approved of by his parents and was desired by them before his birth is a fortunate child indeed. By contrast,
many counselees begin the sad narration of their life
story, "I was a mistake; my parents never wanted me
in the first place." Such a mental hurdle is very difficult
to overcome.

It is a sign of maturity in a parent when he does
*not* react negatively to his child's weaknesses that
parallel his own. Most parent-child personality conflicts
are caused by the parent's reaction to his own weakness
manifested in his child. He hates the thing in himself;
consequently, he despises it in his child and overreacts.
The child should not be expected to understand that
the parent's rejection is not against him personally,
but against those traits that remind him of himself.
As a child, he will interpret the parent's actions as
total rejection.

The mature parent will recognize himself in his
child, emotionally, physically, and mentally. If he has
learned to accept himself, he can easily accept his
child. Once having communicated that acceptance, he
can lovingly help him toward overcoming his weaknesses.

(3) *Avoid anger in the home*—Destructive anger
erupts in many forms, all of which prove harmful to
children, who are so self-centered by nature that parental irritation automatically makes them regard themselves as the cause of the upset and the object of the
anger. Such anger produces an insecure and resentful
child, which as we have seen compounds his negative
behavior and increases his parent's expression of anger.
Young parents in particular are very impatient. When
confronted with the immature and often exasperating
activities of a child, this impatience bursts into harsh
language or angry discipline, which only aggravates
the child's self-rejection and insecurity and prepares
him for self-pity and depression.

(4) *Open display of parental love in the home*—
One of the best things parents can do to promote a
sense of security and love in a child is to demonstrate

love regularly in the home. As a result of the rising divorce rate today, children are forced to choose sides between the two people on earth they love most, mother and father, whose angry outbursts toward each other emotionally confuse the child and cause him to build up defenses against giving himself in love to someone else. If the home disintegrates and he is forced to leave one parent, he may resent the one he accompanies and fantasize about the one he leaves. Remember, the child who watches his mother and father demonstrate affection for each other will develop a pre-disposition toward security, affection, and a good mental attitude.

Looking back on my childhood, I recall being raised during the depression. My father died before my tenth birthday, leaving my twenty-eight-year-old mother a widow with three small children, including my five-year-old sister and my seven-week-old brother. I have never had to deal with a sense of insecurity, largely because I have never known what it is not to be loved. My father had a great capacity to love, and although he was taken from us at an early age, as a child I could understand his absence through death (a sharp contrast to the problem of divorce).

My mother's love for me and her great faith in God always sustained the optimistic idea that no matter what problems arose, a reasonable solution could be found. Every child has a right to such love and acceptance. As I conjure up fond memories of my parents, I especially remembered my father coming into the kitchen, putting his arms around my mother, and lifting her three inches off the floor in a warm, affectionate embrace. That scene always gave me a sense of security. Even the memory of that scene made me feel good. Many of the emotional neuroses children reflect today could probably have been avoided had they experienced such obvious demonstrations of their parents' love.

(5) *Rules for guidelines*—Just as a swinging bridge with guardrails is easier to walk across than the same bridge without protection, so every child needs fences or limits set by his parents to direct his

behavior. These rules should be simple and well-defined, administered with love. They will constantly change with the age of the child, but whenever you set a rule, prepare for the child to test it, and don't expect him to thank you for it. I have watched children chafe at rules, badger their parents about them, and then, when they have forced their parents to revoke the rule, indicate a loss of respect for the parent.

(6) *Discipline—what a relief!*—Too much parental leniency begets undisciplined children. The Bible makes it very clear that if you spare the rod, you will undoubtedly spoil the child. "Foolishness is bound in the heart of a child; but the rod of correction shall drive it far from him" (Prov. 22:15). Educators tell us that knowledge accompanied with emotion provides the surest form of learning. A vigorous spanking or other appropriate form of discipline when delivered in love makes a profound impression on the mind of the child. Yes, he may feel rejected at the time, but every child needs to discover that he cannot do some things in life. If he is not exposed to discipline, he will fail to learn many valuable lessons that he desperately needs to know. In addition, discipline is cathartic. A child can certainly feel true guilt when he, has done wrong; consequently, even though his punishment hurts, it provides a welcome mental relief. That is why children are frequently in a good mood shortly after being disciplined. Those who refuse to discipline their children cheat them out of that much-needed alleviation of conscience.

Roger came to live in our home against my better judgment. Still in our twenties, my wife and I were not prepared to cope with a teenager. But the welfare worker assured us that if we didn't take him, he would be sent to a boys' detention home. Caught in the crossfire of parental hostility, he was assigned to his mother but desperately wanted to live with his father.

We got along fine as long as we let Roger do pretty much as he pleased. Gradually we had to assign him some chores as we did our own children. Day after day he got worse. Wantonly destructive, he refused to comply with our minimal standards, becoming verbally abusive and nasty. Then it happened! When my wife asked him to do the dishes one Sunday afternoon, he refused, sassed her back, and became downright insulting.

One of the things I had learned from my father the hard way was that no man worthy of the title would suffer his wife to be verbally or physically abused by anyone—including his own children. Stepping into the kitchen, I demanded that Roger apologize, but he steadfastly refused. When I gave him a choice between a "spanking and an apology," he said, "You wouldn't dare!" That challenge couldn't be passed up—so I took him into the bedroom and administered the rod of knowledge to the seat of learning.

Within fifteen minutes Roger was out in the kitchen talking affectionately and happily. He even pitched in and helped me dry the dishes. Somehow that spanking taught him we did love him and also cleared his conscience of the heavy load of guilt for his misconduct. Life once again became livable for the whole family.

Contrary to popular opinion, discipline does not crush or stifle a child's spirit when properly administered. Instead, it often creates quite the opposite effect. The child who is disciplined when he is wrong gains the assurance of his parent's love. It is not at all uncommon for the obstreperous child, whose guilt-laden activities make him irrepressible, to become more considerate, obedient, and loving after proper discipline. By contrast the undisciplined child will have difficulty in achieving a sense of acceptance.

One factor about parental discipline should be stressed. Parents absolutely must be united on rules and standards of behavior. The child will naturally work one parent against the other, much to the disruption of the family and the breakdown of effective discipline. Disagreement on principles should never be aired in front of the child, but thoroughly discussed until a united position and joint policy statement can be shared with the child, whether both parents are present or absent. I have seen perfectly normal children, particularly in their teen years, turn into maladjusted monsters because the mother let it be understood that as soon as father went off to work, his rules were no longer enforced. Equally as harmful is the immature father who finds he can win the affection of his children by lowering mother's standards. That is a short-term love that sows the bitter seeds of confusion and rebellion.

(7) *Consistency—thou art a gem!*—The most important part of discipline is consistency. This relates not only to individual problems in the life of one child, but also to equal consideration of all the children in the family. Maintain few rules whose violation results in spanking, but once established, make sure you exact the penalty without hesitation!

(8) *Be fair—no child is perfect!*—Most young people want their day in court. For that reason the parent should project the image that he is willing to discuss the rules. The child always feels better when he has been able to air his feelings in the family court of justice, even when regulations are not altered. Besides, the parent should train his child to reason matters out, not merely respond emotionally.

(9) *Communicating God's love early*—The child raised by Christian parents is most fortunate, for next to parental love, every human being needs to be assured of God's love. Such a message is best communicated by the child's parents early in life. The little Sunday school song, "Jesus loves me, this I know, for the Bible tells me so," sung fervently by young children every week, acts as a source of reassurance to them. In some of their lives, only such reassurance can compensate for the lack of parental love and help to generate a normal attitude toward life.

(10) *Leading your child to Christ when he is young*—Every human being needs to accept Christ as his personal Lord and Savior. The sooner he does that, the better are his chances of avoiding unnecessary pitfalls that induce emotional trauma. He then can develop a mature, confident emotional pattern that helps to prepare him for the uncertain circumstances of life.

(11) *Guarding against negative thinking*—One's

thinking pattern is learned early in life. Watch your child carefully for signs of negativism or defeatism. Foster in him the assurance that he *can* do all things through Christ who strengthens him. Let him understand that today's impossibility may well become tomorrow's achievement. A child must develop the mental attitude espoused by the old adage, "You can learn to do *anything* if you want to bad enough." But a positive approach to life does not just happen; it results from consistent, patient reassurance on the part of the parent.

A child will never benefit from constant criticism or condemnation. In an airport lounge I recently overheard a parent instructing a second grader how to purchase a paper from a coin-operated newsstand. With a leap of joy the child returned with the paper, obviously expecting his father's approval. His smile instantly turned to dismay and fear as his father berated him publicly for being "stupid." It was yesterday's paper! The father had not learned that family unity and personal responsibility are not promoted by public humiliation.

(12) *The malady of griping*—We have already discovered that griping is very harmful, for verbalized criticism has a way of entrenching negative thoughts not only in the mind of the speaker, but also in the mind of all hearers. Children who go about griping are establishing a predisposition for consistent periods of depression. Refuse to allow your children the luxury of cluttering up your house with criticism.

At fifteen one of our children was a professional griper. No matter what the occasion, he could find something critical or negative to say. Nothing ever pleased him. Finally we decided to take some long overdue parental action. On the basis of 1 Thessalonians 5:18 we showed him that his griping was contrary to the will of God. The first thing he said was, "But. . . ." I stopped him and said, "No buts about it! From now on you are not permitted to gripe in this house. We have a happy household here, and we want your help in keeping it that way." Within three weeks we could see definite signs of improvement. That boy today has a different personality than he had then and much better than if we had permitted him to let that habit become more deeply ingrained in his nature.

(13) *The infirmity of self-pity uncorrected*—Self-pity is a natural mental escape pattern for the child who cannot keep up with or compete in an adult world. Even the third child, contending with older brother and sister, tends to struggle with self-pity more than others.

Gentle and consistent instruction in avoiding this tendency will guard the child from a thought pattern that will have to be broken forcibly later in life to avoid depression.

(14) *And be ye thankful*—Every Christian should learn that the spirit of thanksgiving brightens drooping spirits and eliminates depression. Children who are taught to be thankful to God first and then to their parents are well on their way to depression-free living. Teach them early to give thanks for food, love, shelter, health, teachers, and friendship. Children have an amazing ability to learn spiritual truths, and it is often easier for them than for adults to understand that God has a plan even in adverse circumstances. Train your child, "In every thing give thanks" (1 Thess. 5:18), "and when he is old, he will not depart from it" (Prov. 22:6).

(15) *See your child as he is becoming*—Most parents tend to view their children as they *are* rather than as they will *become*. I can remember looking at my sons and wondering whether they would ever amount to anything. Today I am very proud of two young men. When children are little, picture them on your imagination screen as they are becoming, for then you will empathize with them and sense their latent potential. Otherwise the reality of the present may only illuminate a selfish, intemperate, grimy little urchin. Be careful to maintain an attitude of affection and patience, for a child cannot easily distinguish between his parent's displeasure at him or his deed. Happy is the child whose parents recognize that by God's grace he will grow up to be a well-adjusted, successful adult some day.

(16) *Setting a good example*—The best learning tool for any child is the example of his parents. If they see you indulging in negativism, self-depreciation, or self-pity, they will follow suit. But if you manifest practices conducive to winning over depression, your children will imitate those good habits.

Almost every authority on depression, both modern and ancient, observes that depression seems to run in families. We know two reasons for this: inherited temperament and home training. You cannot control the temperament of your child, but you can govern his training. I am inclined to believe that depression runs in families primarily because children tend to copy the bad habits of their parents. I have long observed that depressed children of depressed-prone parents display similar vocabularies and thinking patterns.

Have you ever heard the expression, "When you talk to him, it's just like talking to his father"? Every parent should ask himself, "If my child grows up to think and talk like me, will he manifest a happy spirit and emotional stability or exhibit those symptoms which anticipate depression?"

# 17

# How to Help a Depressed Friend

Depressed people need help! Their erratic behavior notwithstanding, they require the support of those around them even though their actions make it difficult. Some will display an angry or irritable face that rebuffs their friends when they need them most. Many withdraw into silent isolationism, lending the impression that they want to be alone. Don't believe it! Your assistance will be more valuable at that point than at any other time.

Frequently the family of a depressed person, unaware of his depression, becomes exasperated by his behavior. Consequently, when he needs understanding and empathetic love, he may be subjected to unkind words and disapproval, which only compounds his depression. Even when he withdraws, he is really afraid to be alone. Don't expect such a person to reach out for support, but confer it anyway. The Bible teaches that love is kind. If you really love a person, you will befriend him and be considerate of him, not only when he is strong, but when he needs you most—in the chasm of weakness. The following suggestions for extending aid to the depressed will furnish a basic list to which the Holy Spirit will add in light of your own special circumstances. The list is not exhaustive.

(1) *Be there!*—The most important thing you can

do for a depressed person, humanly speaking, is to be present when he needs you. No matter how much he reacts adversely to your presence, he needs you to save him from his self-destructive emotions, mental attitudes and, in some cases, physical violence.

You need not talk or probe or offer advice to be of help. Your presence during a time of intense despondency affords mute evidence of your love and will tend to counteract the rejection that has in one way or another contributed to his depression.

(2) *Don't sympathize with him*—He has slipped into the slough of despond because he has been indulging in self-pity. Don't help him justify his self-pity, but at the same time don't condemn it. He requires understanding and empathy, not condemnation.

(3) *Program hope on the screen of his imagination*—The depressed person universally projects hopelessness and despair, for as we have already seen, his goals have been destroyed, his outlook is negative, and he envisions no solution. For some time his thought patterns have continually concentrated upon failure and hopelessness, thus causing his circumstances to appear many times blacker than they are. Therefore, any kindly and gentle whisper of hope in the face of his present circumstances will be beneficial.

Many times in the counseling room during the first interview, I succeed only in projecting on the depressed person's imagination screen the certainty of hope. If he leaves my office with a ray of hope that someone honestly can foresee an imminent solution to his dilemma, his mental state will probably improve between interviews.

One woman was so convinced of her hopeless condition that she left my office equally as dejected as when she arrived. To my surprise, she returned for her second appointment much improved. Even though she retained no inner confidence, she had been somewhat buoyed up by my confidence that Christ really was her answer and hope was in sight. First she drew strength from my assurance in Christ; then gradually we programmed on the screen of her imagination what He could supply for her. Finally, she began to appropriate the principles of hope for herself through the Word of God.

(4) *Be encouraging but do not argue*—In the midst of programming the hope that is available in Christ, ignore his defense mechanisms of defeatism and negativism and refrain from being excessively positive. He can resent your faith at that moment, so be gentle and understanding.

(5) *Get him to think about something besides himself*—Self-occupation is a hallmark of the depressed. Whenever possible, guide his thinking toward others. One depressed counselee announced that she had found help from the taxi driver on the way to my office. Evidently he was an outspoken, self-pitying character who freely expressed his misery. She admitted, "I feel better just listening to him. He's got more problems than I have."

(6) *Try to engage him in activity*—There is something therapeutic about body motion, for it stimulates the flow of blood, palpitates the heart, and tends to activate the glands. I have found that jogging after a heavy preaching schedule is equally as beneficial as sleeping, and in some cases better. Emotional exhaustion leaves us spent, whereas activity tends to clean out the system. You may wish to foster involvement in your friend's favorite sport or activity as a suggestion to get him started.

(7) *Help him assume his normal responsibilities —gradually*—Everyone faces responsibilities in life, and sooner or later he must resume these responsibilities. Be careful that you do not dump the full load on him at first, because the heavy weight of responsibility may be the original cause for depression.

(8) *Don't be too cheerful!*—The wise man in Proverbs 25:20 states, "As he that taketh away a garment in cold weather, and as vinegar upon nitre [soda], so is he that singeth songs to an heavy heart." A depressed person finds a loud, cheerful person a great source of irritation.

I found this graphically illustrated in my study the day after our church was defeated by the San Diego City Council in our request to build a new church.

A dear missionary friend supported by the church had heard the bad news and came to cheer me up. He wanted to be helpful, but he proceeded injudiciously. With a big smile on his face, he slapped me on the shoulder and laughingly cried, "PRAISE THE LORD!" Strange as it may seem, my reaction was one of intense anger. I not only resented his lack of sensitivity and understanding, but even his cheerful grin. The fact that he was right and I was 100% wrong did not help a bit.

I did not require sympathy, but was in need of understanding. He gave me neither. One must attempt to cheer up a depressed person graciously, gently, tenderly, and slowly.

(9) *Get him into the Word of God*—Nothing relieves a depressed person more than rehearsing the promises of God. Unfortunately, his depression makes him resentful of God, and thus he avoids the only solution to his emotional problem. If he will permit you to read portions from the Word, do so. Offer him suggestions as to key portions *he* could read, like some of the great psalms of David, who experienced depression and knew how to cure it. Suggest also that he read some good book which you can personally recommend. It is my hope that this book will become a therapeutic tool which many can present to their depressed friends.

(10) *Pray with him in a thankful spirit*—Even the depressed will rarely refuse prayer, which they usually recognize as their last hope. But make sure that you pray to God *about* them and their problem, not *at* them. Remember, you are extremely vulnerable at this moment, for your prayer will reveal your understanding of his problem. Be very careful not to condemn him for his resentment and self-pity. Let the Holy Spirit do the work of conviction, and also pray with thanksgiving for what God has done and is able to do in his life. Just hearing your prayer of thanksgiving and understanding can be therapeutic.

(11) *Spend time with him*—The Bible teaches that the first characteristic of love is patience, meaning endurance. If you really love a person, confirm that

love when he is depressed by spending time with him, affording reassurance that someone really loves him.

## Helping Those in the Despair of Grief

The death of a loved one naturally induces grief. This is even true of the warmest-hearted Christian. Many times I have heard Christians admit after the loss of a loved one, "You can never really prepare yourself for death." Although that is certainly true, Christians do not "sorrow as those without hope."

First Thessalonians 4:13-18 was written to a young church to dispel their sadness at the loss of loved ones. The comfort of that passage is founded on the promise that we shall see our believing loved ones again. That is one of the treasured truths in the Bible. Because Jesus Christ is coming again, all those who trust Him will be reunited some day. A person who realistically programs that fact on the screen of his imagination will sharply reduce the tragedy of grief. The pain of bereavement cannot be removed immediately, but it will gradually diminish.

A non-Christian at the time of grief is most difficult to console, for he is "without Christ and without hope in this world." Sometimes such individuals will cry out to God in their desperation and be saved. Whatever their plight, they need companionship, for being alone becomes the worst feature of their experience at this time. Fortunately, an intuitive consciousness of this fact exists in almost every human being, which explains why relatives and loved ones rush to the side of a person who has just lost a partner, parent, or child. We all recognize a common need at such a time.

Assistance to a grieving individual includes rehearsing for him the promises of God. Under severe grief it is not uncommon for the mind to go blank. Thus a friend who spends time with him, providing reassurance of God's promises and faithfulness, will be a tremendous inspiration. It takes love, love, and more love to be that kind of friend.

# 18

# The Miserable Majority

"Why art thou cast down, O my soul? and why art
thou disquieted in me? hope thou in God" (Ps. 42:5).

Sooner or later everyone is depressed! One's
mental condition may not be severe enough to have
him hospitalized in a catatonic state or so despairing of
life as to attempt suicide, but he will inevitably encounter depression sometime.

For most people depression is a transient experience that overtakes them when the circumstances of
life hit a low ebb at the same time their spiritual battery
is down and their mental thinking pattern is negative.
Usually the depression passes within a limited time
provided the person straightens out his spiritual life,
as previously explained, and changes his thinking pattern toward himself, the  problem, or the person causing the problem. To eliminate the depression, it is not
necessary to change the problem, but it is essential to
adjust the mental attitude.

Hopefully the person will not have made some
major decision during the depression that will compound his circumstances, such as running away from
home, getting a divorce, quitting school, or leaving a
job. Usually it is dangerous to make a major life decision when you are depressed. It is preferable to eliminate the depression first, then proceed to the decision.

For many people, depression is a way of life. They learned the habits of resentment and self-pity early and consequently have developed a well-entrenched thought process that needs changing. Such individuals should be encouraged by the fact that although depression creates a good deal of misery, it need not be fatal. In fact, a close examination of the Bible reveals that some of the greatest servants of God had no small problem with depression. If the old adage is true that "Misery loves company," depressed people will enjoy this chapter.

## Job the Patient

One of the greatest men in the ancient world was the patriarch Job. Some feel he was a contemporary of Abraham, and therefore he lived about 400 years before Moses. Some historians believe he may have been the mastermind behind the construction of the pyramids of Egypt.

In the early years of Job's life he was exceedingly blessed of God. Among his assets were seven sons and three daughters, 7,000 sheep, 3,000 camels, 1,000 oxen, 500 donkeys and "a very great household." No wonder the Scriptures say, ". . . this man was the greatest of all the men of the east."

Naturally Job had no problem with depression in those days—not with everything going well for him. But suddenly all that changed. His animals were stolen or slain and a tornado destroyed the home of his oldest son during a party, killing all his children. To make matters worse, his body was covered with boils "from the sole of his foot unto his crown."

Although Job did not realize he was being tested by God to prove his genuine faithfulness, throughout all this tragedy he did not sin, even when his wife encouraged him to "curse God and die!" His positive reaction to all this tragedy, which would have plunged the average person into the pit of despair, has earned him the reputation of being the world's most patient man.

Everyone has his breaking point, however, even

Job. The final straw occurred when his three best friends came over to encourage him to confess the sin in his life that brought on this series of tragedies. After sitting on the ground in silence for several days, Job spoke. His words clearly reveal depression, for he had finally indulged in the sins of resentment and self-pity. A careful reading of chapters 3 and 7 bear this out. Some of his thoughts indicating his self-pity are as follows:

3:1 "Job opened his mouth, and cursed his day."

3:3 "Let the day perish in which I was born. . . ."

3:4 "Let that day be darkness; let not God regard it from above, neither let the light shine upon it."

3:6 "As for that night, let darkness seize upon it; let it not be joined unto the days of the year, let it not come into the number of the months."

3:10 "Because it shut not up the doors of my mother's womb, nor hid sorrow from mine eyes."

3:11 "Why died I not from the womb?"

Only a heart of solid granite would find it difficult to understand Job's sinful response, but that does not excuse or mitigate it. This great man was depressed by the same sinful mental attitude that causes today's depression—self-pity. When he confessed his sin (7:20, 21), indicating that he had maintained his faith in God in spite of his awful tragedy, Job was forgiven and his spirits lifted. He then entered into a debate with his friends attesting to the faithfulness of God. Job's increasing spirit and faith are apparent in chapters 9 through 41, *before* his circumstances improved. As a result, God blessed Job with "twice as much as he had before" (42:10). Not only were his riches restored, but he and his wife were granted seven more sons and three beautiful daughters. In addition, long life and health were bestowed upon Job, who lived 140 more years and saw four generations of his sons.

The primary lesson to learn from Job is not only that we must rejoice in spite of unbelievably tragic circumstances, but that even when we don't at first, it is still possible to gain forgiveness by looking to God in faith. He is always faithful to His children, for He knows how much we can bear even if we don't. God does not carry a grudge just because we react improperly at first, but is ever ready to forgive and restore.

Job was used mightily of God *after* his time of depression.

## The World's Greatest Leader

When judged by his personal achievement and the impact he made on humanity, Moses stands as the greatest leader in all of history. He not only led three million griping Jews out of Egypt and continued with them for forty years in the wilderness, but he also served as the instrument of God, giving to the world the highest law code and standard of ethics ever produced.

In a previous chapter Moses' self-pitying prayer recorded in Numbers 11:10-15 was used as a classic illustration of harmful prayer. In verse 15 he became so depressed that he asked God, ". . . kill me, I pray thee. . . ." Fortunately for Moses and the children of Israel, God ignored that request, but that he would ask is evidence that his sin of self-pity must have been habitual. A careful review of his life likewise indicates a serious problem with anger or resentment. Put these two sins together and you have the perfect formula for depression.

The fact that Moses' self-pity and consequent depression was forgiven and God continued to use him for thirty-eight more years again illustrates that depression need not be fatal. A depression-prone person can be used of God if he will repent of his evil thinking pattern and trust Him for the future. This is particularly true if the biblical principles for living are firmly established in his mind so that in a fit of depression he does not make a serious blunder that will so ensnarl his life that after the depression is past he becomes a "castaway" and is no longer usable for God's perfect will in his life.

Another great leader who came on the world scene about twelve centuries after Moses offers a good example by contrast. Having triumphed over the western world by the time he was thirty-three years old, Alexander the Great became depressed because there were no more worlds for him to conquer. During his depression he turned to drink, and it is said that he literally drank himself to death. Moral values and biblical principles for living as found in the Bible, when programmed into the filing cabinet of the mind, will keep such tragedies from occurring.

## The Father of the Prophets

Next to Moses, Elijah was probably the greatest man in the Old Testament, possessing miraculous power in order to heal the sick, raise the dead, prevent rain for three years, and even call down fire from heaven. On one occasion he single-handedly killed 450 evil prophets of Baal who had committed the worst sin known to man—deceiving men about God. He established the school of the prophets which was used mightily of God to keep Israel and Judah from going into paganism and idolatry sooner than they did.

Even though he was a great man of God, Elijah also knew the defeat of depression. On one occasion he became so despondent that he asked God to let him die (1 Kings 19:4).

Rather fanciful suggestions have been offered by some Bible teachers in an attempt to justify his depression: "The psychological letdown after the public confrontation with the prophets of Baal on Mt. Carmel," "He was discouraged with the children of Israel because so many of them had gone to worshiping Baal," or "Queen Jezebel was after him and she had a vicious reputation." Like modern-day excuses, however, they are nothing more than intellectual meringue —all froth and no substance. Elijah was depressed merely because he was indulging in self-pity! First Kings

19:10 shows his thinking pattern clearly: "I have been very jealous for the LORD God of hosts: for the children of Israel have forsaken thy covenant, thrown down thine altars, and slain thy prophets with the sword; and I, even I only, am left; and they seek my life, to take it away."

As a matter of record, 7,000 other prophets were true to God. But in Elijah's mind he was the only faithful one left. Self-pity always blinds one's eyes to resources and maximizes difficulties.

Who has escaped such thoughts? "I am the only one who has to do this chore." "I am the only person who can't sing." "Mom and dad always pick on me, never the others." Such disobedient thinking ultimately produces depression which will continue until the thinking pattern changes.

Fortunately for Israel, and for Elijah, he repented of his sin, the Lord protected him, and he outlived both Jezebel and her wicked husband, King Ahab.

## The Disgruntled Prophet

If the number of souls converted to Christ through a man's preaching were the measure of greatness, the prophet Jonah has to be recognized as the greatest preacher of all time. It is estimated that over one million Ninevites repented as a result of his preaching.

Instead of being elated at the way God used him to bring salvation to so many people, this prophet became strangely depressed. He actually prayed, "O LORD, take, I beseech thee, my life from me; for it is better for me to die than to live" (Jonah 4:3).

A secular counselor would understandably probe for some deep-seated emotional problem in Jonah's life to account for this depressed state. Some might even attribute it to the emotional letdown that followed his frenetic preaching schedule. But the simple fact remains that Jonah was "displeased exceedingly" and "very angry!" He was angry at God because He had forgiven the sins of the Ninevites and spared their lives. Jonah hated the Ninevites! His hatred was not without human justification, of course, for they had cruelly persecuted the children of Israel for years. He probably was overjoyed that God was finally going to destroy them, which no doubt is why he originally refused to go there and preach to them. So when God forgave them, his fury was unrestrained. His anger led to self-pity and ultimately to such a state of depression that he asked God to let him die. What an example of turning an undeniably joyous occasion into a depressing experience! Jonah should have trusted God for the outcome which he did not understand. Instead, his self-pity short-circuited his potential for rejoicing, so he withdrew into the anguish of seclusion, muttering to himself and complaining to God.

We may be tempted to excuse Jonah, for the New Testament command, "In every thing give thanks" (1 Thess. 5:18), had not yet been written, but you can be sure that if he had thanked God for the great spiritual revival in Nineveh, he would never have been depressed.

## The Weeping Prophet

Some men rose out of the pages of history at a time when the most appropriate service to perform for their nation was to weep. Jeremiah lived at such a time! And he wept. And his tears were justified. Israel, the great nation once blessed of God, had so apostatized that she had been led away captive 135 years before. Only a spiritual revival under King Hezekiah and the prophet Isaiah had saved Judah. To this southern tribe had fled all the faithful children of Israel for safety. In spite of the mighty hand of God in delivering this little nation, her children eventually forgot the God of their fathers. To such a nation God called Jeremiah, the weeping prophet.

With deep concern and open weeping, he warned the people that if they did not repent of their sins and return to God, the Babylonians would destroy their city and lead them away captive. Instead of appreciating his honest warnings and exhortations to repent in order to avoid the impending judgments of God, the people turned unmercifully on Jeremiah. He was imprisoned several times and on one occasion was placed in stocks. Although he responded in the Spirit most of his life, at one time he was obviously depressed—as demonstrated in his prayer life. In the 15th chapter of the book which bears his name we find a prayer that establishes the depth of his self-pity. "Woe is me, my mother, that thou hast borne me a man of strife and a man of contention to the whole earth! I have neither lent on usury, nor men have lent to me on usury; yet every one of them doth curse me" (15:10).

Finally he turned on the Lord and erupted with this tragic outburst, "I sat not in the assembly of the mockers, nor rejoiced; I sat alone because of thy hand: for thou hast filled me with indignation. Why is my pain perpetual, and my wound incurable, which refuseth to be healed? wilt thou be altogether unto me as a liar, and as waters that fail?" (vv. 17, 18). The Lord responded to Jeremiah, ". . . they shall fight against thee, but they shall not prevail against thee: for I am with thee to save thee and to deliver thee. . . . And I will deliver thee . . . out of the hand of the terrible" (vv. 20, 21).

God seems to understand when His children lapse into self-pity, particularly when the pressures of life become too heavy. But that does not exempt them from the depression which naturally follows. Jeremiah accepted God's assurances that "I am with thee to save thee . . ." and went on to serve God many years. In fact, his external condition grew worse, but he looked to God and avoided a recurrence of his depression.

We can all profit by the lesson Jeremiah learned through this difficulty reflected in one of his short prayers: "Thy words were found, and I did eat them; and thy word was unto me the joy and rejoicing of mine heart" (15:16). The best source of joy for the depressed child of God comes through looking to the Lord in His word.

# 19

# An Eighty-Five-Year-Old Optimist

"In every thing give thanks: for this is the will of God in Christ Jesus concerning you" (1 Thess. 5:18).

It isn't often that one meets a genuine optimist in life, particularly one who is eighty-five years old. A contemporary of Moses and Joshua, this man's infectious faith makes him a classic illustration of the principles of this book. To my knowledge, not one negative thing is recorded about this great man. Although he had ample reason to indulge in self-pity, it seems evident that he never did, even as an octogenarian. In addition to a vital faith in God, he possessed an exceedingly positive mental attitude and vision that everyone should imitate. If they would, I am confident the seventies would be known as a decade of optimism rather than as "the decade of depression."

## My Favorite Character

The exploits of hundreds of great men are recorded in the Bible. The one who stands head and shoulders above them all is the little-known man of God named Caleb. Although not listed in the New Testament "Who's Who" of Hebrews 11, this man and his optimistic spirit should inspire everyone interested in studying people.

The first time he appears in the pages of Holy Writ, the nation Israel was facing a crucial test. The Lord had led them out of Egypt, spoken to them at Sinai, and brought them to the southern border of the land He had promised to give them. To encourage His people, God instructed Moses to select a leader from each of the 12 tribes "that they may search the land of Canaan" (Num. 13:2).

## The Godly Spy

Caleb was forty years old and a leader of his tribe when selected to go in and spy out the land. Commissioned to discover the strength of their adversaries, the location of their cities and strongholds, and the condition of the land, he did his work well. Not content to bring back merely a verbal report, he and his friend Joshua, Moses' chief lieutenant, returned with some of the fruit of the land, including grapes so large that a giant bunch was carried on a pole between two men.

Upon their return to Kadesh-barnea, where the people waited for the report, a great crowd gathered around them. To Caleb's amazement, ten of the spies presented a very negative report. In spite of the fruitfulness of the land flowing "with milk and honey," they were more impressed with the strength and size of the opposition.

Unbelief has a strange way of magnifying difficulties and minimizing resources. In addition, it is contagious! The ten faithless spies summed up their report about the giants in the land by saying, "We be not able to go up against the people; for they are stronger than we . . . and we were in our own sight as grasshoppers, and so we were in their sight" (Num. 13:31, 33).

This "evil report" of the ten faithless spies reveals a common malady of unbelief for it underestimated their own abilities, overexaggerated the prowess of the enemy, and totally ignored God's power and continued direction in the affairs of Israel. Consequently, they came to a negative conclusion entirely unrelated to the facts. This tendency seriously limited God's use of their lives and jeopardized the lives of their families.

Caleb leaped up and "stilled the people before Moses, and said, Let us go up at once, and possess it; for we are well able to overcome it. . . . If the LORD delight in us, then he will bring us into this land, and give it us; a land which floweth with milk and honey" (Num. 13:30; 14:8).

Unfortunately for Israel, the people believed the negative report of the majority instead of the faithful testimony of Caleb and Joshua. Consequently, instead of possessing their inheritance, they were banished to a forty-year sojourn in the wilderness. Of all the adults living at that time, only Caleb and Joshua were permitted to enter the land thirty-nine years later. The rest perished in the wilderness because of their unbelief!

## Forty-Five Years Later

When the time finally came for the children of Israel to possess the land of Canaan, even the great leader Moses was dead. Joshua, his successor, led the new generation of Isarelites into the land God had promised them. Contrary to popular misconception, taking the land away from the giants was no easy matter. In fact, it took six years of fierce fighting before the twelve tribes found it safe to establish their dwellings in the land. Under Joshua's direction, Caleb had been an active leader during those awful years of war.

One day, near the close of the fighting, the two survivors of the wilderness wanderings were walking together. Caleb reminded his old friend Joshua of the promise Moses had given him forty-five years before: "Surely the land whereon thy feet have trodden shall be thine inheritance, and thy children's for ever, because thou hast wholly followed the LORD my God. And, now, behold, the LORD hath kept me alive, as he said, these forty and five years, even since the LORD spake this word unto Moses, while the children of Israel wandered in the wilderness: and now, lo, I am this day fourscore and five years old. As yet I am as strong this day as I was in the day that Moses sent me: as my strength was then, even so is my strength now, for war, both to go out, and come in. Now therefore give me this mountain, whereof the LORD spake in that day; for thou heardest in that day how the Anakims were there, and that the cities were great and fenced: if so be the LORD will be with me, then I shall be able to drive them out, as the LORD said" (Josh. 14:9-12). Caleb knew when he made his request that all the remaining giants in the country had fled to this mountain, but that did not daunt his eighty-five-year-old spirit one bit. Though his enemies were well-entrenched and had made the mountain a stronghold of giants, he said, "Give me this mountain." He knew his God was well able to deliver it to him—and He did!

The Bible does not tell us how old Caleb was when he died, but the inference is that he lived many years on his mountain. In fact, he probably cleared off a beautiful view where he could look out over the land below.

## The Secret of Caleb's Mental Attitude

If self-pity can ever be justified, humanly speaking, Caleb was certainly entitled to indulge in that sin. Banished to chewing dust out in the wilderness for thirty-nine years because of someone else's sins, he could have turned out to be a notorious griper. He could have spent his time thinking, "If those unbelieving people had listened to Joshua and me, we could have been settled in the land when I was in my prime." Every time a dust storm blew up, he could easily have blamed his plight on the unbelievers.

Interestingly enough, not one self-pitying or griping word is written of him. Instead, he fathered several children and together with his wife raised them to serve the Lord. And throughout those years he had his goal set on one day building his home on that beautiful mountain he had seen as a forty-year-old spy. He didn't know how he would do it, but he had absolute confidence that eventually God would fulfill His promise.

Even though he had to wait forty-five years, he not only found God faithful, but he finally experienced the "exceedingly abundant blessing" for which our God is famous.

The real secret to Caleb's greatness appears in God's description of him as "my servant Caleb" who "had *another spirit* with him, and hath followed me fully" (Num. 14:24). That other spirit that characterized Caleb obviously means the Holy Spirit, the hallmark of any Spirit-filled, obedient, trusting Christian. You can have that same spirit. It it certainly *God's will for your life.*

Be sure of this, the spirit of Caleb that so valiantly shielded him from depression is available to you. If, like Caleb, you learn the primary spiritual lesson in the face of emotional pressure, "In everything give thanks," whether you understand the circumstances of life or not, looking forward to God's ultimate deliverance from your problem, you will never again be defeated by depression. It is entirely up to you!

# Bibliography

Adams, Jay E., *Competent to Counsel*. Nutley, N.J.: Presbyterian and Reformed Publishing Company (1971).

Adolph, Paul E., *Release from Tension*. Chicago: Moody Press (1956).

Arieti, Silvano, ed., *American Handbook of Psychiatry*, 2 vols. New York: Basic Books (1959).

Beck, Aaron T., *Depression: Causes and Treatment*. Philadelphia: University of Pennsylvania Press (1967).

Berne, Eric, *Games People Play*. New York: Bantam Books (1972).

———, *What Do You Say After You Say Hello?* New York: Bantam Books (1972).

Brandt, Henry R., and Homer E. Dowdy, *Christians Have Troubles, Too*. Old Tappan, N.J.: Fleming H. Revell Company (1968).

Cammer, Leonard, *Up From Depression*. New York: Pocket Books (1971).

"The Campus Life Forum: Does This Girl Look Like a Witch?" *Campus Life*, XXX (January, 1973), 12-14ff.

Christenson, Larry, *The Christian Family*. Minneapolis: Bethany Fellowship (1970).

Collier, Robert, *The Secret of the Ages*, rev. ed. Tarrytown, New York: Robert Collier Publications (1951).

"Coping With Depression," *Newsweek,* LXXI (January 8, 1973), 51–54.

Dobson, James, *Dare to Discipline*. Wheaton, Illinois: Tyndale House Publications (1970).

Haggai, John Edmund, *How to Win Over Worry*. Grand Rapids: Zondervan Publishing House (1959).

Hallesby, O., *Temperament and the Christian Faith*. Minneapolis: Augsburg Publishing House (1962).

Harris, Thomas A., *I'm OK—You're OK*. New York: Harper and Row (1967).

Hart, Hornell, *Chart for Happiness*. New York: Macmillan Company (1940).

Hildebrand, Kenneth, *Achieving Real Happiness*. New York: Harper and Brothers (1955).

Hyder, O. Quentin, *The Christian's Handbook of Psychiatry*. Old Tappan, N.J.: Fleming H. Revell Company (1971).

Jabay, Earl, *The God-Players*. Grand Rapids: Zondervan Publishing House (1969).

Koch, Kurt E., *Christian Counseling and Occultism*. Grand Rapids: Kregel Publications (1965).

La Haye, Tim, *Spirit-Controlled Temperament*. Wheaton, Ill.: Tyndale House (1966).
———, *Transformed Temperaments*. Wheaton, Ill.: Tyndale House (1971).

Lindsey, Hal, *Satan Is Alive and Well on Planet Earth*. Grand Rapids: Zondervan Publishing House (1972).

Lloyd-Jones, D. Martyn, *Spiritual Depression: Its Causes and Cure*. London: Pickering and Inglis (1965).

McMillen, S. I., *None of These Diseases*. Old Tappan, N.J.: Fleming H. Revell Company (1963).

Maltz, Maxwell, *Psycho-Cybernetics and Self-Fulfillment*. New York: Bantam Books (1970).

Murphy, Joseph, *"The Power of Your Subconscious Mind*. Englewood Cliffs, N.J.: Prentice-Hall, Inc. (1963).

Nelson, Marion H., *Why Christians Crack Up*. Chicago: Moody Press (1960).

"New Drug Helps Manic Patients," *San Diego Union*, June 22, 1973, p. A8.

Osborne, Cecil, *The Art of Understanding Yourself*. Grand Rapids: Zondervan Publishing House (1967).

Ostow, Mortimer, *The Psychology of Melancholy*. New York: Harper and Row (1970).

Saparina, Y., *Cybernetics Within Us*. Hollywood: Wilshire Book Company (1967).

Schuller, Robert H., *Self-Love: the Dynamic Force of Success*. New York: Hawthorn Books (1969).

Schwartz, David J., *The Magic of Thinking Big*. New York: Cornerstone Library (1959).

Solomon, Charles R., *Handbook of Happiness*. Denver: Grace Fellowship Press (1971).

Stevenson, George S., and Harry Milt, *Master Your Tensions and Enjoy Living Again*. Englewood Cliffs, N.J.: Prentice-Hall, Inc. (1959).

Szasz, Thomas S., *The Myth of Mental Illness*. New York: Dell Publishing Company (1961).

Tournier, Paul, *The Healing of Persons*. New York: Harper and Row (1965).

Wilson, Margery, *Kinetic Psycho-Dynamics*. Englewood Cliffs, N.J.: Prentice-Hall, Inc. (1963).

"Your Emotional Stresses Can Make You Sick," Chicago *Tribune*, July 18, 1972, Section 1, p. 1ff.

## ABOUT THE AUTHOR

DR. TIM LAHAYE has been a counselor for more than twenty-five years. He is the senior minister of two dynamic churches in San Diego and El Cajon, California, and is president and founder of Christian Heritage College. In addition to *How to Win Over Depression*, he is also the author of *Spirit-Controlled Temperament*, *How to Be Happy Though Married*, *Transformed Temperaments*, *The Beginning of the End* and the recently completed *Revelation—Illustrated and Made Plain*.